AMERICA'S
PAST AND PROMISE

Geography Resources

McDougal Littell Inc.
A Houghton Mifflin Company
Evanston, Illinois   Boston Dallas Phoenix

To the Teacher

This geography booklet, for use with *America's Past and Promise*, provides valuable resources for strengthening students' map and geography skills and for teaching the five geographic themes. The booklet consists of two main parts: (1) map practice activities and (2) geography challenge activities.

- **Map practice activities,** one per textbook chapter, are each accompanied by an outline map. Students are asked to label on these outline maps significant places that are mentioned in the chapter. The questions are designed to give students practice in basic map skills.

- A **geography challenge activity** is also provided for each textbook chapter. These activities extend and enrich concepts that are taught in the textbook. In addition to reinforcing map and graph skills, these worksheets require students to utilize such critical thinking skills as inferring, drawing conclusions, comparing and contrasting, and determining cause and effect.

Answers for worksheets are found at the back of the booklet. Students' answers for questions that call for interpretations, opinions, and judgments will of course vary. For such questions, notes concerning appropriate bases for answers are printed.

Maps: Mapworks, Cleveland Design

Cover design: Corey McPherson Nash
Cover image: Tony Rinaldo (eagle: Tom and Pat Leeson)
Inset photo credit: © Tom Van Sant/Geosphere Project, Santa Monica/Science Photo Library/Photo Researchers Inc.

Printed in the U.S.A.

ISBN: 0–395–70763–3

45678910–B–99 98 97 96

Contents

UNIT 1   A New Atlantic World

Chapter 1 The First Americans
Map Practice: Early Migration to the
    Americas 1
Outline Map 1 2
Geography Challenge: Indian Culture
    Areas in 1500.. 3

Chapter 2 Peoples of West Africa
Map Practice: Landforms of Africa.................. 5
Outline Map 2 6
Geography Challenge: Empires of West
    Africa... 7

Chapter 3 Europeans Reach Outward
Map Practice: The Voyages of Columbus 9
Outline Map 3 10
Geography Challenge: Viking Routes............. 11

Chapter 4 Spain Builds an Empire
Map Practice: Routes of Spanish Explorers
    in North America...................................... 13
Outline Map 4 14
Geography Challenge: Spain in North
    America.. 15

UNIT 2   Colonial Settlement

Chapter 5 Challenges to Spanish Power
Map Practice: European Exploration of
    North America... 17
Outline Map 5 18
Geography Challenge: Roanoke Colony 19

**Chapter 6 English Colonies in North
    America**
Map Practice: The Thirteen English
    Colonies.. 21
Outline Map 6 22
Geography Challenge: Colonial Immigrant
    Groups, 1770 23

**Chapter 7 Shaping of the American
    Colonies**
Map Practice: Triangular Trade Routes.......... 25
Outline Map 7 26
Geography Challenge: The Colonies at
    Work 27

Chapter 8 The Clash of Empires
Map Practice: Mississippi River Drainage
    Basin 29
Outline Map 8 30
Geography Challenge: Changing Land
    Claims in North America........................... 31

UNIT 3   A New Nation

Chapter 9 The Thirteen Colonies Rebel
Map Practice: Proclamation of 1763 33
Outline Map 9 34
Geography Challenge: British Control
    Over Colonial Trade 35

Chapter 10 Americans Win Independence
Map Practice: North America, 1783 37
Outline Map 10 38
Geography Challenge: The Siege of
    Yorktown 39

Chapter 11 Creating the Constitution
Map Practice: The Original Thirteen
    States 41
Outline Map 11 42
Geography Challenge: Ratifying the
    Constitution.. 43

UNIT 4   Building the Nation

Chapter 12 Launching a New Government
Map Practice: Launching a New
    Government 45
Outline Map 12 46
Geography Challenge: The Nation's
    Capital 47

**Chapter 13 Expanding and Defending
    Boundaries**
Map Practice: Appalachian Crossings............. 49
Outline Map 13 50
Geography Challenge: The United States,
    1803.. 51

Chapter 14 The Expanding Nation
Map Practice: National Confidence and
    Economic Expansion 53
Outline Map 14 54
Geography Challenge: King Cotton................. 55

UNIT 5   Expansion and Change

Chapter 15 The Age of Jackson
Map Practice: The Age of Jackson 57
Outline Map 15 58
Geography Challenge: The Election of
    1828.. 59

Chapter 16 Changes in American Life
Map Practice: Immigration in the
    Mid-1800s 61
Outline Map 16 62
Geography Challenge: The Underground
    Railroad 63

Chapter 17 The Westward Movement
Map Practice: Trails Across the West 65
Outline Map 17 66
Geography Challenge: The United States
    Gains Land from Mexico 67

UNIT 6   The Nation Divided and Rebuilt

Chapter 18 The Nation Breaking Apart
Map Practice: Steps to Civil War 69
Outline Map 18 70
Geography Challenge: Fort Sumter Falls 71

Chapter 19 The Civil War
Map Practice: The Civil War 73
Outline Map 19 74
Geography Challenge: Railroads and the
    Civil War 75

Chapter 20 Rebuilding the South
Map Practice: The Election of 1876 77
Outline Map 20 78
Geography Challenge: The Economic
    Effects of the Civil War 79

UNIT 7   America Transformed

Chapter 21 An Industrial Society
Map Practice: Railroads in 1900 81
Outline Map 21 82
Geography Challenge: Work Stoppages,
    1890–1895 83

Chapter 22 The Rise of American Cities
Map Practice: Growth of Cities in the
    Great Lakes Region 85
Outline Map 22 86
Geography Challenge: Immigration,
    1820–1920 87

Chapter 23 Forces Shaping a New West
Map Practice: Cattle Trails and Cow
    Towns 89
Outline Map 23 90
Geography Challenge: Land Regions of the
    West 91

Chapter 24 Politics and Reform
Map Practice: Politics and Reform 93
Outline Map 24 94
Geography Challenge: Growth of Cities,
    1860–1900 95

Chapter 25 Becoming a World Power
Map Practice: Expansion in Latin
    America 97
Outline Map 25 98
Geography Challenge: The Panama Canal 99

UNIT 8   Troubled Decades

Chapter 26 The Roaring Twenties
Map Practice: The United States in the
    1920s 101
Outline Map 26 102
Geography Challenge: The Palestine
    Mandate 103

**Chapter 27 The Depression and the
    New Deal**
Map Practice: The Great Depression 105
Outline Map 27 106
Geography Challenge: The Growth of
    Farm Tenancy 107

Chapter 28 A More Diverse America
Map Practice: Americans, 1900–1940 109
Outline Map 28 110
Geography Challenge: Immigration
    Restrictions in the 1920s 111

**Chapter 29 The Rise of Dictators and
    World War II**
Map Practice: The Allies Win in Europe 113
Outline Map 29 114
Geography Challenge: The North African
    Campaign 115

UNIT 9   A Changing America

Chapter 30 The Cold War Era
Map Practice: The Vietnam War 117
Outline Map 30 118
Geography Challenge: Communist
    Governments After World War II 119

Chapter 31 Postwar America
Map Practice: Population Shift,
    1950–1970 121
Outline Map 31 122
Geography Challenge: Shifting Centers
    of Population 123

Chapter 32 The Search for Equal Rights
Map Practice: The Civil Rights
    Movement 125
Outline Map 32 126
Geography Challenge: School Integration,
    1954–1960 127

**Chapter 33 Patterns in Our Recent
    History**
Map Practice: The Middle East 129
Outline Map 33 130
Geography Challenge: The World After
    the Cold War 131

Answers 133

CHAPTER 1
Early Migration to the Americas

Map Practice
Geography Worksheet 1

A. Use the map on textbook page 6 to locate the following features. Label these features on the Outline Map on the back of this page.

Continents	*Bodies of Water*	*Other Features*
Europe	Pacific Ocean	Beringia
Asia	Atlantic Ocean	Ice Sheet
North America	Arctic Ocean	
South America	Bering Sea	

B. Use the maps on textbook pages 6 and R14–R15 to answer the following questions.

1. From which continent did early people migrate to the Americas? Draw their routes on

   the Outline Map. _____

2. Name two ways that scientists think Paleo-Indians may have migrated to the Americas.

   (See textbook, page 6.) _____

   _____

3. Which two mountain ranges might people migrating to South America have crossed?

   _____

4. Which continents did Beringia connect? _____

5. What caused Beringia to disappear? (See textbook, page 6.) _____

   _____

6. What body of water exists today where Beringia once was? _____

7. Explain how the domestication of plants changed the way people in the Americas lived.

   (See textbook, page 7.) _____

   _____

   _____

   _____

   _____

CHAPTER 1: Outline Map

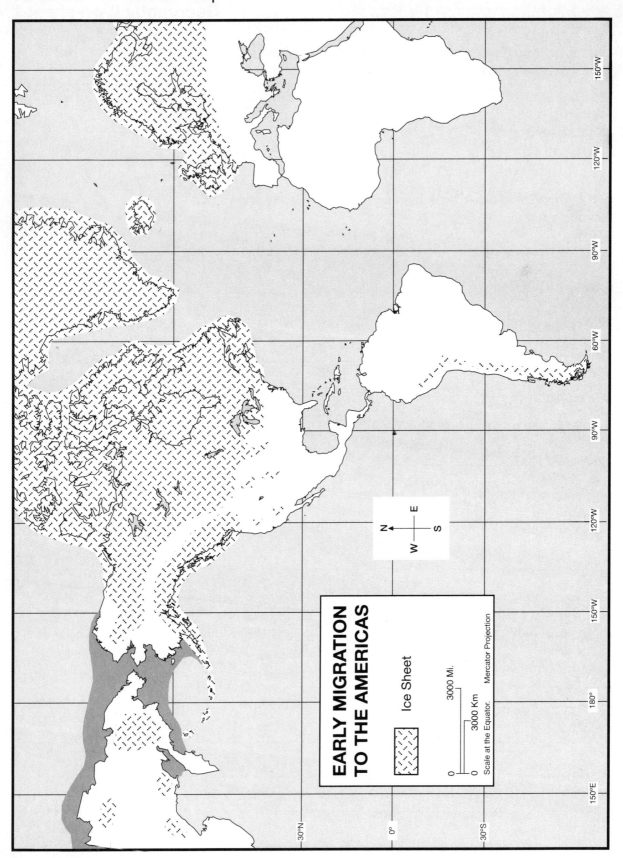

EARLY MIGRATION
TO THE AMERICAS

Ice Sheet

3000 Mi.

3000 Km

Scale at the Equator.   Mercator Projection

AMERICA'S PAST AND PROMISE

Name _____   Date _____

CHAPTER 1
Indian Culture Areas in 1500

The map below shows the different culture areas found in the
Americas in 1500. Use this map with the maps on textbook
pages 17 and R14–R15 to answer the questions that follow.

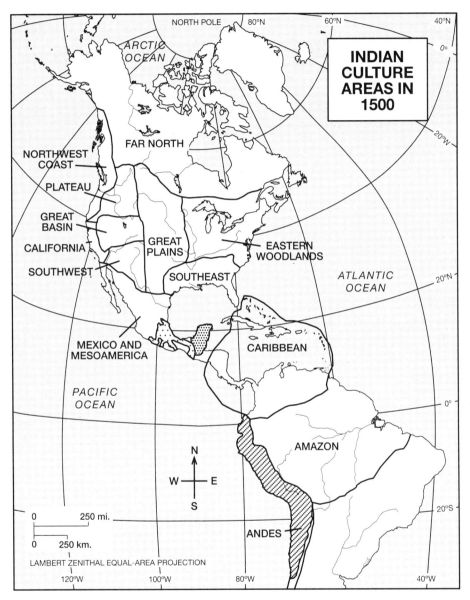

1. According to the map, which groups lived in the Far North culture area? _____

   _____

2. In which culture area did the Algonquin live? _____

3. Through which three culture areas did the Mississippi River flow? _____

   _____

Name _____

4. Which culture areas surrounded the Gulf of Mexico? _____

_____

5. Which three culture areas were found in South America? _____

_____

6. Where were the Aztec Empire and the Maya Empire located? Label these empires on

the map above. _____

7. Where was the Inca Empire located? Label it on the map above. _____

8. In which culture area did the Modoc live? _____

9. Geographic Theme: Regions How did the geography of the Northwest Coast determine the lifestyle of the people there? (See textbook, page 15.)

_____

_____

_____

_____

_____

_____

_____

_____

_____

_____

CHAPTER 2   Map Practice
Landforms of Africa   Geography Worksheet 3

A. Use the map on textbook page 28 to locate the following continents and features. Label these continents and features on the
Outline Map on the back of this page.

Continents	*Bodies of Water*		*Other Features*
Africa	Atlantic Ocean	Niger River	Sahara
Europe	Mediterranean	Zambezi River	Sudan
Asia	Sea	Senegal River	Kalahari Desert
	Indian Ocean	Congo River	Atlas Mountains
	Red Sea	Orange River	Congo Basin
	Gulf of Guinea	Lake Victoria	Arabian
	Nile River		Peninsula
			Great Rift Valley

B. Use textbook pages 27–29 to answer the following questions.

1. What is the Sahara? Where is it located? _____

2. Where did most early humans in Africa live? _____

3. What impact did the drying of the Sahara have on the people who lived there?

   _____

   _____

4. Around what large river did Africans heading east out of the Sahara settle?

   _____

5. What was the first culture of the Nile Valley? _____

6. How did Nubians make their living? _____

   _____

7. How did the use of caravans help make Kush a strong center of trade? _____

   _____

8. How did Africans south of the Sahara make their living? _____

   _____

CHAPTER 2: Outline Map

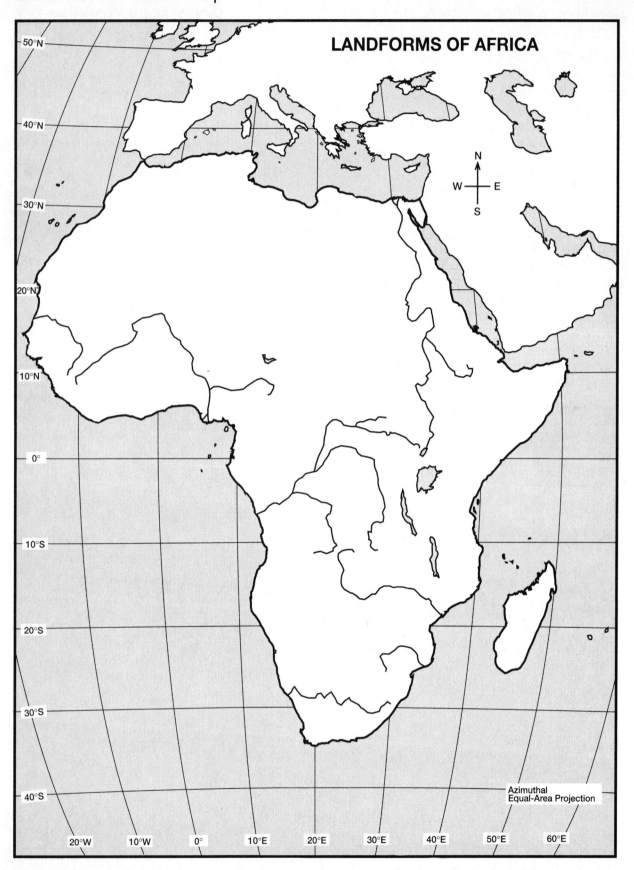

LANDFORMS OF AFRICA

N
W   E
S

Azimuthal
Equal-Area Projection

Name _____   Date _____

Between the 300s and 1500s, three empires relied on the gold-salt trade for their wealth and survival. The control of land made this trade possible. When enemies pressed at the borders, however, the each empire went into decline. Study the maps of the West African empires below. Then answer the questions that follow.

EMPIRES OF WEST AFRICA

1. According to the map, which empires reached the Atlantic Ocean?

   _____

   _____

2. Which empire extended farthest east? _____

   _____

3. Which empire covered the smallest area? _____

   _____

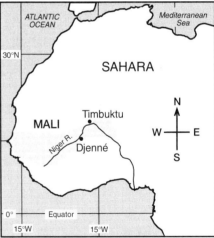

4. Which empire extended farthest north? _____

   _____

5. In which empire was the city of Timbuktu located? What features made this city famous?

   _____

   _____

   _____

6. Why was salt important to the people living in West Africa? (See textbook, page 30.)

   _____

   _____

   _____

7. How did Islam spread into Africa? (See textbook, page 31.) _____

_____

8. What impact did the spread of Islam have on the African slave trade? (See textbook,

page 31.) _____

_____

9. Geographic Theme: Movement Why did more and more West Africans come to
accept Islam? Explain. (See textbook, page 35.)

_____

_____

_____

_____

_____

_____

_____

_____

CHAPTER 3
The Voyages of Columbus

Map Practice
Geography Worksheet 5

A. Use the map on textbook page 53 to locate the following features.
Label them on the Outline Map on the back of this page.

Bodies of Water	*Continents*	*Islands*	*Voyages*	*Other Places*
Atlantic Ocean	North America	Cuba	Voyage of 1492	Palos
Pacific Ocean	South America	Hispaniola	Voyage of 1493	Spain
Caribbean Sea	Europe	San Salvador	Voyage of 1498	Central
	Africa		Voyage of 1502	America

B. Use the map on textbook page 53 to answer the following questions.

1. From which continent, country, and city did Columbus begin his voyages?

_____

2. In which major direction did Columbus sail across the Atlantic to the New World? Back

to Spain? _____

3. Which two islands did Columbus explore on his first voyage? _____

4. Which trip took Columbus the farthest south and which continent's mainland did he

reach? _____

5. Which island did Columbus and his crew explore on their third voyage? _____

6. During which voyage did Columbus explore part of the coastline of Central America?

_____

Use textbook pages 51–54 to help you answer question 7.

7. What did Columbus learn on his voyage to Africa that later helped him succeed?

_____

_____

_____

CHAPTER 3: Outline Map

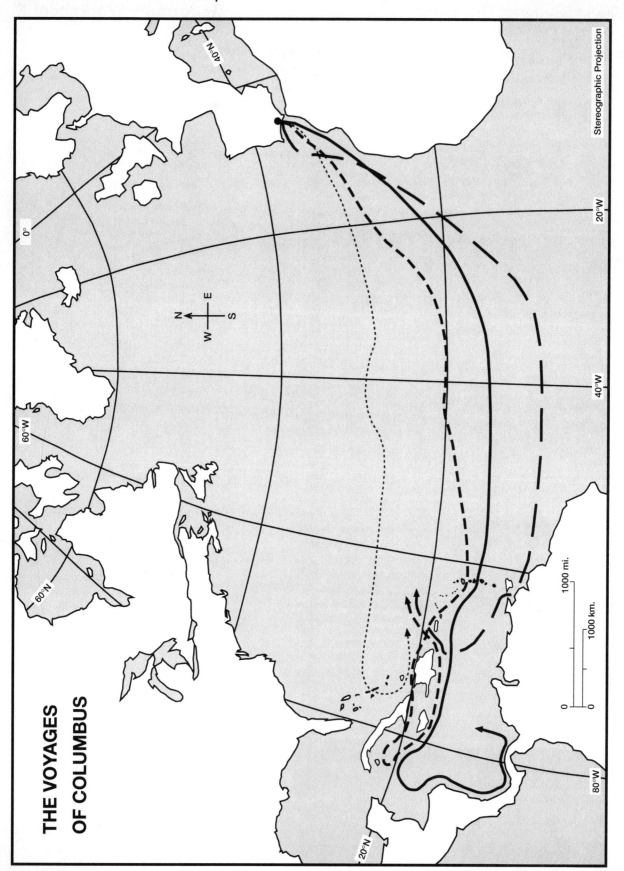

THE VOYAGES
OF COLUMBUS

Stereographic Projection

AMERICA'S PAST AND PROMISE
© Houghton Mifflin Company. All rights reserved.

Name _____ Date _____

In the ninth and tenth centuries, Viking invaders posed a threat
to European kingdoms. Vikings also sailed west across the
Atlantic Ocean and explored the coast of North America in about
A.D. 1000. The map below shows the route the Vikings followed.
Use the map to answer the questions that follow.

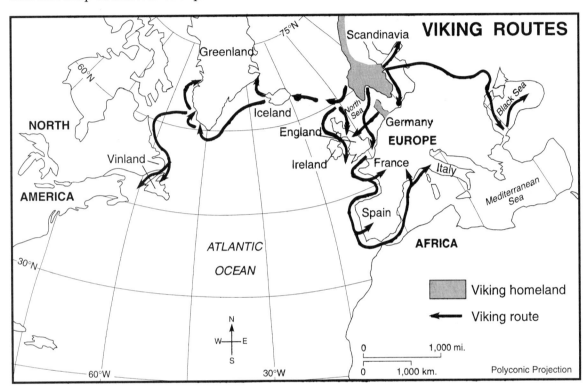

1. Which three modern countries make up the Viking homeland? (See textbook, page 44.)

_____

2. In what three main directions did the Vikings sail from their homeland?

_____

3. Based on the map, why might you conclude that the Vikings were a seafaring people?

_____

_____

_____

4. Into what bodies of water did the Vikings sail? _____

_____

5. Which countries of western Europe did the Vikings invade? _____

_____

_____

_____

6. In about A.D. 870, Vikings began to settle an island in the North Atlantic, located just south of the Arctic Circle about 650 miles west of the Scandinavian coast. What is the name of that island?

_____

7. In terms of latitude, about how far north did the Vikings travel? _____

8. From what large island did the Vikings set out to explore the coast of North America?

_____

9. Geographic Theme: Movement Describe the impact the Viking invasions had on western Europe. (See textbook, page 44.)

_____

_____

_____

_____

_____

_____

_____

_____

CHAPTER 4   **Map Practice**
Routes of Spanish Explorers in North America   **Geography Worksheet 7**

A. Use the map on textbook page 75 to locate the following bodies of
water, islands and other places, and routes of Spanish explorers.
Label these features on the Outline Map on the back of this page.

Bodies of Water	*Land Areas*	*Routes of Explorers*
Atlantic Ocean	North America	Ponce de León
Gulf of Mexico	Mexico	De Soto
Pacific Ocean	Florida	Coronado
Mississippi River	California	Cabeza de Vaca
Rio Grande		Cabrillo
Arkansas River		

B. Use the map on textbook page 75 to answer the following questions.

1. Which Spanish explorer sailed from Puerto Rico around the coast of Florida?

_____

2. Which explorer sailed down the Mississippi River? _____

3. Which two explorers traveled northward from Mexico to the present-day United States?

_____

4. Describe the route of Cabeza de Vaca from the Gulf of Mexico to Culiacán.

_____

_____

5. According to this map, which Spanish explorer traveled the farthest northward?

_____

6. Which two explorers traveled mainly by water? _____

7. Through which bodies of water did Narváez sail? _____

  Trace his route on your Outline Map. Which explorer continued his expedition?

_____

Use the Atlas map on pages R14–R15 of your textbook to answer
the following question.

8. Which explorers traveled through the Great Plains? _____

_____

CHAPTER 4: Outline Map

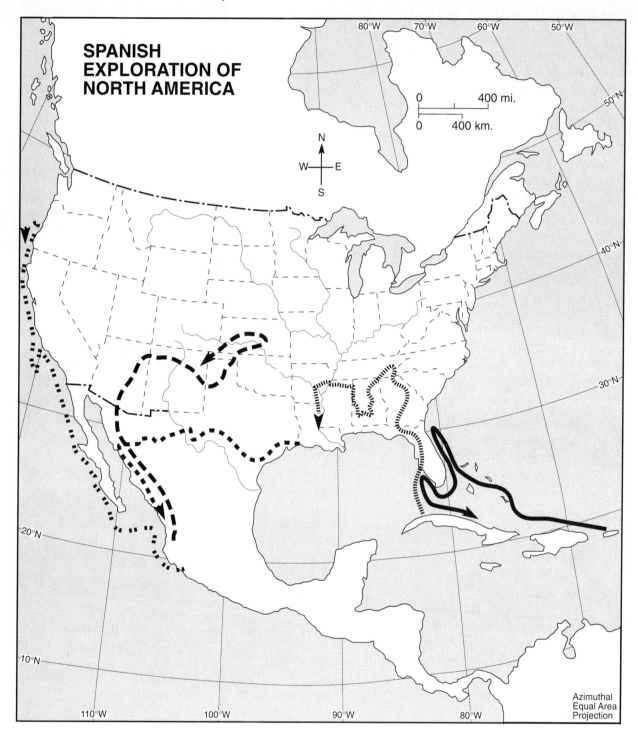

SPANISH
EXPLORATION OF
NORTH AMERICA

CHAPTER 4
Spain in North America

Spain considered its period of settlement in North America a glorious one. The Indian inhabitants had reason to see it differently. Study the map and graph below and answer the questions that follow.

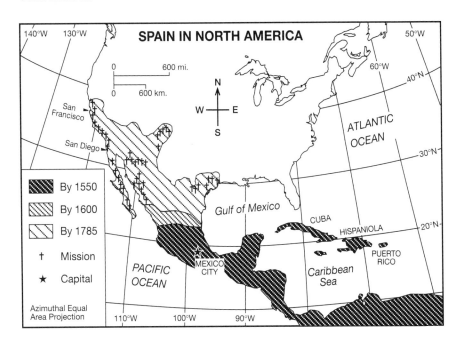

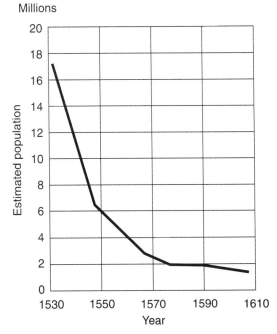

Decline in Population of Central Mexico
1532–1608

Source: Borah and Cook, *The Aboriginal Population of Central Mexico on the Eve of the Spanish Conquest*

1. In which compass direction did Spain's conquest of North America proceed?

   _____

2. The Spanish capital in North America was Mexico City. Use a ruler and the scale bar to determine the distance from Mexico City to San Francisco.

   _____

3. Which areas of North America did Spain settle first? Which did it settle last?

   _____

   _____

   _____

   _____

4. Spain had three **traditions that enabled it to settle a land rapidly:** it was a nation of sea-farers, conquerors, and rulers of outside territories. Which fourth tradition, judging from the map, aided Spain's colonization of the Americas? Explain.

_____

_____

_____

5. What happened to the Indian population of Central Mexico as the Spanish moved north-

ward? _____

6. By what date had the Spanish conquered the Aztec capital of Tenochtitlán and founded

Mexico City? _____

7. What happened to the Indian population of Central Mexico during that same period?

_____

8. During which twenty-year period did the Indian population of Central Mexico fall by

about four million? _____

9. Geographic Theme: Movement Why did the Spanish continue to move north? Why did their movement have a disastrous impact on the Indian people already living in North America?

_____

_____

_____

_____

_____

_____

_____

CHAPTER 5
European Exploration of North America

Map Practice
Geography Worksheet 9

A. Use the maps on textbook pages 92 and R14–R15 to locate the following features. Label them on the Outline Map on the back of this page.

Bodies of Water	*Settlements*	*Routes of Explorers*
Atlantic Ocean	Quebec	Cartier
Lake Huron	Roanoke	Champlain
Lake Erie		Hudson
Lake Ontario		Verrazano
Hudson River		
St. Lawrence River		

B. Use the map on textbook page 92 to answer the following questions.

1. Which explorer sailed farthest north? _____

2. Which explorer sailed northward along the Atlantic coast? _____

3. Which two explorers traveled along the St. Lawrence River? _____

4. Which of the Great Lakes did Champlain explore? _____

5. Describe the route Hudson took on his first voyage to North America.

_____

6. From what country or countries did each of the following explorers sail?

   a. Hudson _____

   b. Verrazano _____

   c. Champlain _____

   d. Cartier _____

7. What was each of the explorers listed above searching for? (See textbook, pages 91–93.)

_____

8. Read the clues and answer the question "Who am I?" (See textbook, pages 91–93.)

   a. I opened the way for Dutch colonists to settle present-day New York.

   WHO AM I? _____

   b. I founded the first permanent French settlement in North America.

   WHO AM I? _____

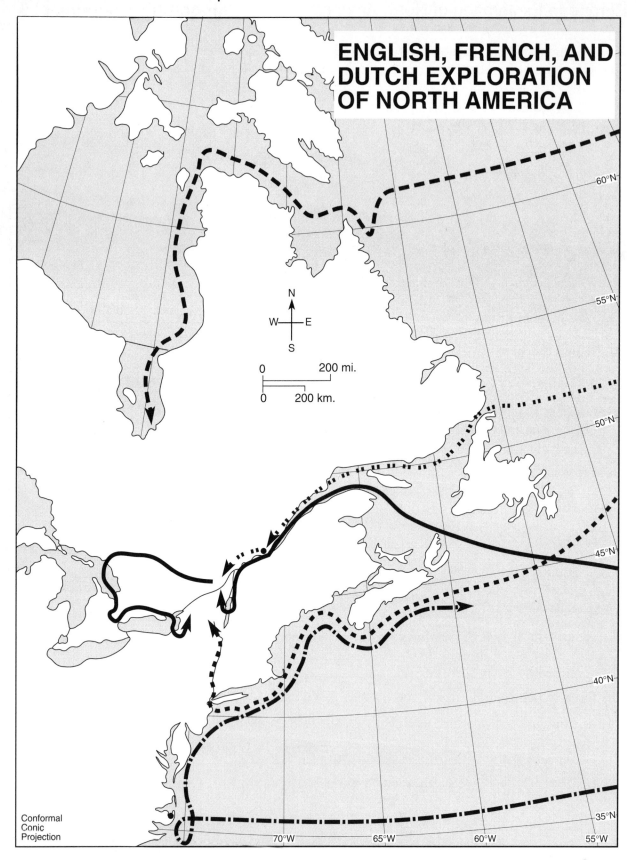

ENGLISH, FRENCH, AND DUTCH EXPLORATION OF NORTH AMERICA

Name _____   Date _____

North America's Atlantic coast provided many good sites for
European settlement. Offshore islands and sandbars protect the
coast from ocean storms. The continuous motion of the sea push-
es sandbars toward the shore, however. The area near the shore
often fills in with saltwater marshes, which make poor sites for
settlement. The map below shows the site of Roanoke Island
Colony off the coast of present-day North Carolina. Use the map
to answer the questions that follow.

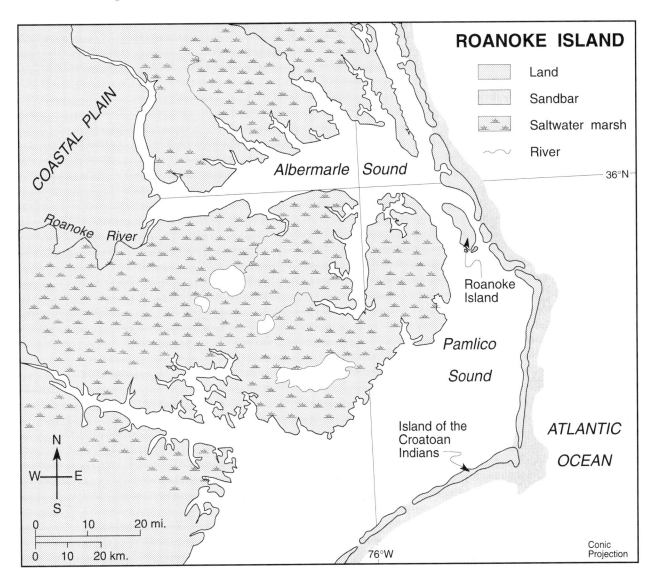

1. Who sponsored the first English colony in the Americas? _____

2. What is the approximate latitude of Roanoke Island? _____

In which direction is Roanoke Island from the island of the Croatoan Indians?

_____

3. What body of water separates Roanoke Island from the Island of the Croatoan Indians?

_____

4. What landforms are located east of Roanoke Island? _____

5. What kind of land makes up the mainland nearest Roanoke Island? _____

6. Use the map's scale bar to determine the approximate distance from Roanoke Island to

the mouth of the Roanoke River. _____

7. What serious deficiency made Roanoke Island a poor site for a settlement? (See text-

book, page 103.) _____

_____

8. Geographic Theme: Place What advantages and disadvantages did the site of
Roanoke Island have for English settlers? What lessons did the English learn from their
failure at Roanoke? (See textbook, page 103.)

_____

_____

_____

_____

_____

_____

_____

_____

CHAPTER 6
The Thirteen English Colonies

Map Practice
Geography Worksheet 11

A. Use the map on textbook pages 122 and R14–R15 to locate the following bodies of water, colonies, and other features. Label them on the Outline Map on the back of this page.

Bodies of Water	*Colonies*		*Other Features*
Atlantic Ocean	Massachusetts	New Jersey	Appalachian
Lake Superior	(2 locations)	Delaware	Mountains
Lake Michigan	New Hampshire	Maryland	Spanish Territory
Lake Huron	Rhode Island	Virginia	French Territory
Lake Erie	Connecticut	North Carolina	
Lake Ontario	New York	South Carolina	
	Pennsylvania	Georgia	

B. Use the map on textbook page 122 to answer the following questions.

1. Which colony was located between the two parts of Massachusetts? _____

2. Which town on the map was settled earliest? Which was settled latest? Give the date

   each was settled. _____

3. The Pilgrims had planned to settle near the mouth of the Hudson River (later the site of New York City). Use a ruler and the scale bar to determine about how many miles off course they were when they landed at Plymouth.

   _____

4. Which physical feature provided a natural barrier against the western expansion of the colonies?

   _____

5. How did the English gain control of New York? (See textbook, page 122.) _____

   _____

6. What religious group settled in Pennsylvania? What were their beliefs? (See textbook,

   pages 122–123.) _____

   _____

7. Which nation would probably have objected to the English exploration of the Great

   Lakes region? Of Florida and the Gulf Coast? Explain. _____

   _____

CHAPTER 6: Outline Map

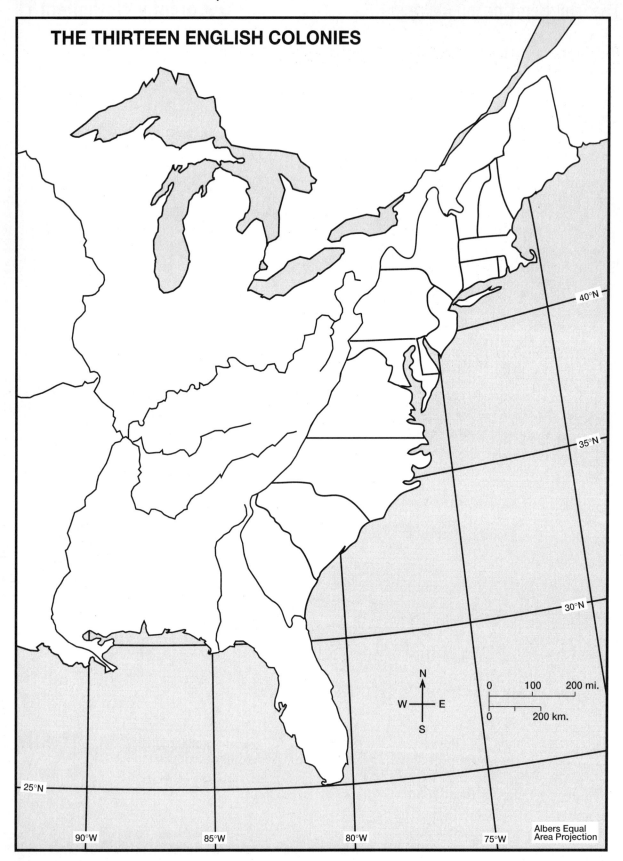

THE THIRTEEN ENGLISH COLONIES

40°N

35°N

30°N

N
W   E
S

0   100   200 mi.

0   200 km.

25°N

90°W   85°W   80°W   75°W

Albers Equal
Area Projection

CHAPTER 6
Colonial Immigrant Groups, 1770

Geography Challenge
Geography Worksheet 12

By 1770 people from several European countries and from Africa
lived in the English colonies. European immigrants tended to live
near people with the same national background. Africans, who
were brought to the colonies as slaves, lived in those colonies
whose agricultural economies depended most heavily on slave
labor. The map below shows where immigrant groups settled.
Study the map and key and answer the questions that follow.

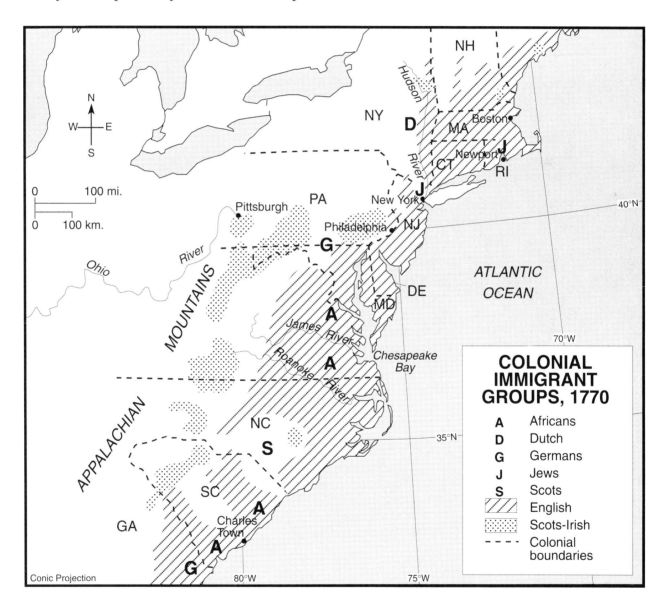

1. Which two groups of immigrants were found in large numbers throughout the colonies?

_____

2. Which group settled farthest west? _____

3. Which group settled in New York City and in Newport, Rhode Island? _____

4. Where did the Dutch settle? _____

5. According to the map, in what colonies did German immigrants settle? _____

_____

6. In what colony did Scots immigrants settle? _____

7. Based on the map, which colonies had the largest number of Africans?

_____

8. Geographic Theme: Regions Explain how settlement by different groups of people can affect the development of regions. Use examples from the settlement of the English colonies. (See textbook pages 114–123.)

_____

_____

_____

_____

_____

_____

_____

_____

CHAPTER 7
Triangular Trade Routes

A. Use the map on textbook page 138 and the Atlas in the back of your book to locate the following body of water, continents, countries or colonies, and cities. Label these features on the Outline Map on the back of this page.

Body of Water	*Continents*	*Countries/*	*Cities*
Atlantic Ocean	Europe	*Colonies*	Boston
	Africa	Britain	New York
	North America	West Indies	Philadelphia
	South America	English Colonies	Charles Town
			(Charleston)

B. Use the information on textbook pages 137–138 to answer the following questions.

1. What three places made up the **triangular trade route** represented by the red line on the

   map? _____

2. What did the colonies send to Africa? _____

3. Where were slaves and gold from Africa sent? _____

4. What was sent from the West Indies to the English colonies? _____

   _____

5. Across what body of water did these **triangular** trade routes run?

   _____

6. Based on the map, what was the shortest leg of the triangular trade routes?

   _____

7. In which direction did ships sail from the West Indies to England? _____

8. In which direction did ships sail from the West Indies to the colonies? _____

9. Which American cities were important ports? _____

   _____

CHAPTER 7: Outline Map

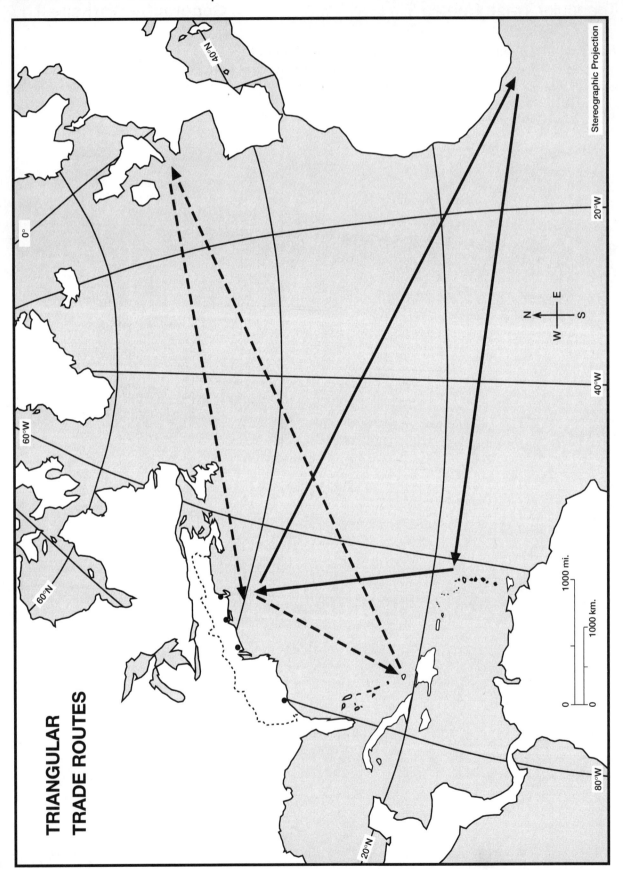

TRIANGULAR
TRADE ROUTES

Stereographic Projection

40°N

20°W

0°

40°W

60°W

N
W   E
S

60°N

1000 mi.

1000 km.

80°W

20°N

Name _____ Date _____

In the American colonies, the characteristics of the land helped define the type of economy of each region. Study the three maps below and answer the questions that follow.

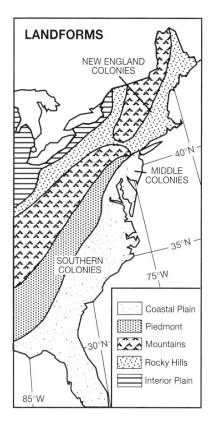
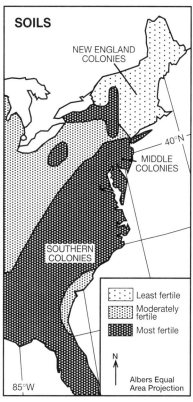
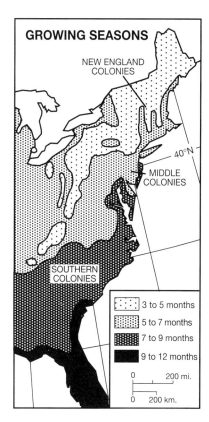

1. Which region had the longest growing season? _____

2. Which region had the least fertile soil? _____

3. In which region did most of the Coastal Plain lie? _____

4. What is the name of the mountain range shown on the landforms map? (Refer to the map of United States physical features on textbook pages R14–R15.)

   _____

5. Between which two landforms does the Piedmont lie? _____

   _____

6. What industries did New Englanders develop to make up economically for their hilly land, poor soil, and short growing season? (See textbook, pages 136–137.)

   _____

7. Which region depended largely on slave labor to support its plantations? _____

_____

8. Geographic Theme: Regions Many factors affect how people use their land. Use the
maps on the previous page to explain why the New England Colonies prospered from
whaling, fishing, and shipbuilding industries, and the Southern Colonies prospered from
an economy based on agriculture.

_____

_____

_____

_____

_____

_____

CHAPTER 8   **Map Practice**
Mississippi River Drainage Basin   **Geography Worksheet 15**

A. Use the maps on textbook page 156 and pages R14–R15 to locate
the following bodies of water, mountains, and settlement. Label
these features on the Outline Map on the back of this page.

Bodies of Water			*Mountains*	*Settlement*
Gulf of Mexico	Lake Superior	Illinois River	Appalachian	New Orleans
Lake Ontario	Mississippi R.	Ohio River	Mountains	
Lake Erie	Platte River	Arkansas River	Rocky	
Lake Huron	Red River	Missouri River	Mountains	
Lake Michigan	Wisconsin R.			

B. Use the map on textbook pages 156 and R14–R15 to answer the
following questions.

1. Which two natural features form the boundaries of the Mississippi River drainage basin

   on the east and west? _____

2. Into what body of water does the Mississippi river system empty?

   _____

3. Which river is the longest tributary of the Mississippi? _____

4. In what general direction does the Ohio River flow? _____

5. Which part of the drainage basin is larger, the part east of the Mississippi River or west

   of the river? _____

6. Use the map scale to estimate the length of the Mississippi River. _____

7. Marquette and Joliet followed the Mississippi River as far south as which tributary?

   (See textbook, page 155.) _____

8. Name two tributaries that join the Mississippi north of the Missouri River.

   _____

9. What is the absolute location (latitude and longitude) of New Orleans?

   _____

10. What is the location of New Orleans relative to the Mississippi River? _____

   _____

CHAPTER 8: Outline Map

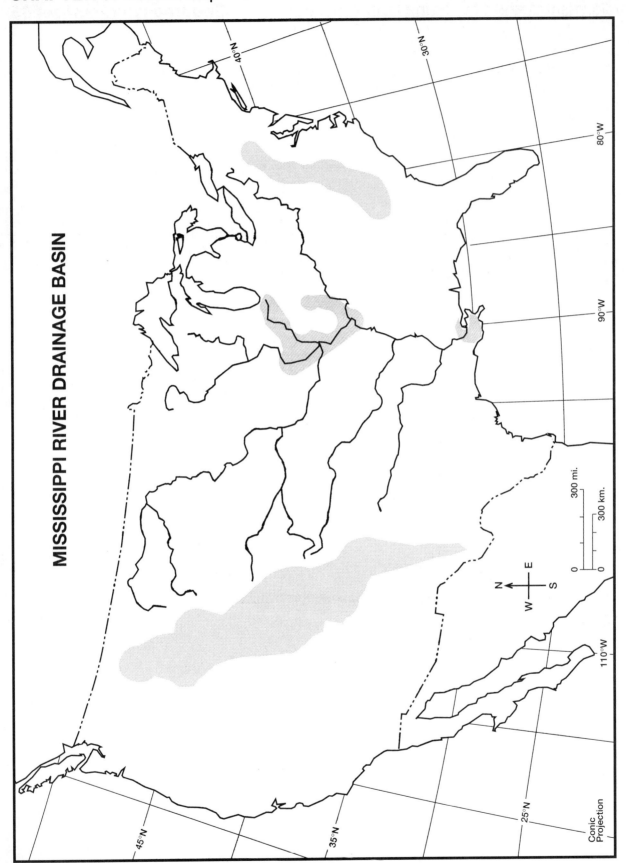

MISSISSIPPI RIVER DRAINAGE BASIN

AMERICA'S PAST AND PROMISE

Name _____ Date _____

CHAPTER 8
Changing Land Claims in North America

In the early 1700s three European powers controlled North America. Rivalry among these powers led to global conflicts. As a result of the French and Indian War (1754–1763), European land claims in North America changed dramatically. Study the two maps below to see what changes took place. Then answer the questions that follow.

CHANGING LAND CLAIMS IN NORTH AMERICA

1713   1763

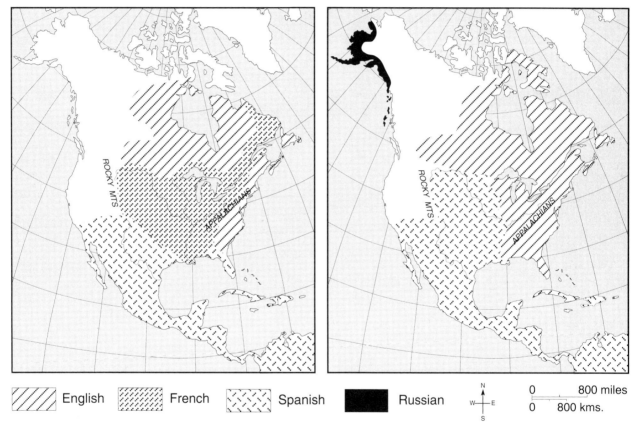

English   French   Spanish   Russian

0 ___ 800 miles
0 ___ 800 kms.

Write before in front of statements that were true in 1713, before the French and Indian War. Write after in front of statements that were true in 1763, after the French and Indian War. Write both in front of statements that were true both in 1713 and in 1763.

_____ **1.** England controlled the Hudson Bay area.

_____ **2.** France claimed the Mississippi, Ohio, and St. Lawrence river valleys.

_____ 3. Russia claimed land along the shores of Alaska.

_____ 4. Florida belonged to Spain.

_____ 5. England controlled the land as far west as the Mississippi River.

_____ 6. France controlled land between the Mississippi River and the Rocky Mountains.

_____ 7. French claims separated England's territory along the Atlantic coast from England's northern territory.

_____ 8. England and Spain both claimed land near the mouth of the Mississippi River.

9. **Geographic Theme: Place** What geographic advantages did England gain in North America as a result of the Treaty of Paris (1763), which ended the French and Indian War? (See textbook, page 167.)

_____

_____

_____

_____

_____

_____

_____

_____

Name _____ Date _____

A. Use the map on textbook pages G8, 122, and 176 to locate the following bodies of water and colonies. Label these features on the Outline Map on the back of this page.

Bodies of Water		*Colonies*		*Other Features*
Atlantic Ocean	Lake Huron	Massachusetts	Delaware	Proclamation
Mississippi	Lake Michigan	New Hampshire	Maryland	Line, 1763
River	Lake Ontario	Rhode Island	Virginia	
Ohio River	Lake Superior	Connecticut	North Carolina	
Lake Erie		New York	South Carolina	
		New Jersey	Georgia	
		Pennsylvania		

B. Use the map on textbook page G8 and your Outline Map to answer the following questions.

1. Which colony was farthest north? _____

2. Which colony was farthest south? _____

3. What geographic feature formed the eastern boundary of the thirteen colonies?

_____

4. What feature marked the western boundary of British claims shown on this map?

_____

5. What line marked the western limit of lands colonists were allowed to settle? (See textbook, pages 175–176.) _____

6. What land was reserved for Indians? _____

7. What bodies of water shown on the Outline Map were located on land reserved for

Indians? _____

8. Where were most British forts located? _____

9. Why did colonists resent the Proclamation of 1763? (See textbook, pages 175–176.)

_____

_____

_____

CHAPTER 9: Outline Map

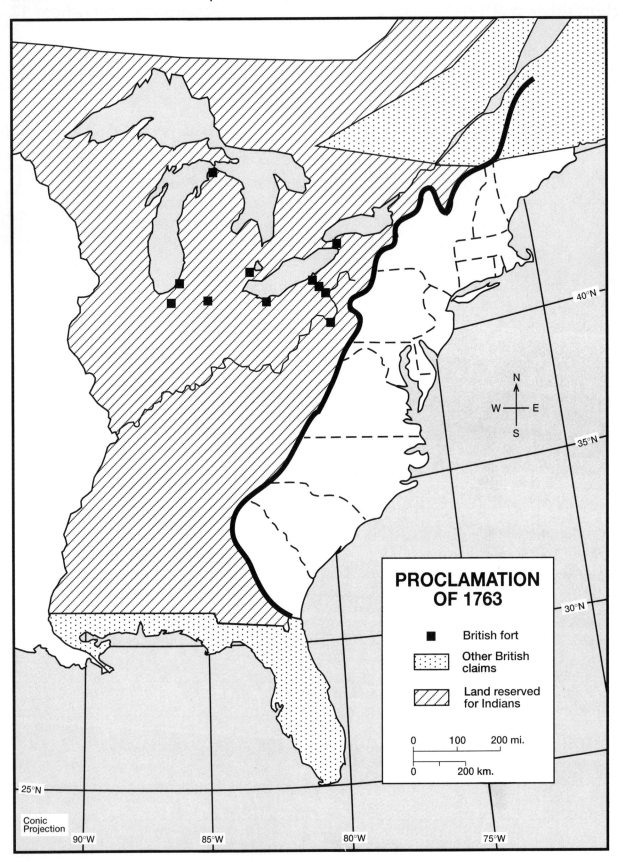

PROCLAMATION OF 1763

- ■ British fort
- Other British claims
- Land reserved for Indians

0   100   200 mi.

0   200 km.

Conic Projection

Name _____   Date _____

The economy of the thirteen colonies depended on trade.
Britain's trade laws restricted imports and exports of important
products. Study the map and chart below and answer the questions that follow.

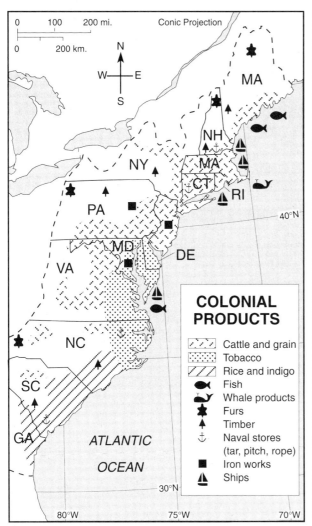

BRITISH CONTROL OVER COLONIAL TRADE	
Exports	
No restrictions	rice, fish, meat
Restricted to England and to English colonies	furs, tobacco, naval stores, indigo, timber
Prohibited	all manufactured goods
Imports	
Permitted from English colonies	iron and most other raw materials
Permitted only from England	manufactured goods such as textiles and hardware; foreign goods (required to pass through English ports before proceeding to colonies)
Prohibited	most goods coming directly from foreign countries and non-English colonies

COLONIAL PRODUCTS

Cattle and grain
Tobacco
Rice and indigo
Fish
Whale products
Furs
Timber
Naval stores (tar, pitch, rope)
Iron works
Ships

1. Which colonies produced rice and indigo? _____

_____

2. Which colonies produced tobacco? _____

_____

3. What goods did Massachusetts produce? _____

_____

4. What colonial goods could be exported without restrictions? _____

_____

5. What goods could colonies export to other colonies? _____

_____

6. What goods could colonies import from other colonies? _____

_____

7. What exports were prohibited? _____

_____

8. Geographic Theme: Movement Describe how British control affected the movement of goods to and from the thirteen colonies.

_____

_____

_____

_____

_____

_____

_____

CHAPTER 10
North America, 1783

Map Practice
Geography Worksheet 19

A. Use the map on textbook page 215 to locate the following bodies of water, countries, territories, and claims. Label these features on the Outline Map on the back of this page.

Bodies of Water	*Countries*	*Territories and*
Hudson Bay	United States	*Claims*
Atlantic Ocean	Canada	Spanish Territory
Gulf of Mexico	Mexico	British Territory
St. Lawrence River		French Territory
Ohio River		Claimed by Britain,
Mississippi River		Spain, and Russia

B. Use the map on textbook page 215 to answer the following questions.

1. Which nation claimed a portion of the new southwestern United States? _____

2. Which nations claimed the area of the northern Pacific coast? _____

3. Look at the area labeled *Boundary uncertain*. Which countries disputed this area?

_____

Use the map on textbook page 215 with the Atlas maps on pages R12–R13 and R14–R15 to help you answer questions 4-6.

4. Which natural feature or features formed boundaries of the following: **a)** most of the northern limit of the United States in 1783; **b)** the eastern limit of Spanish Territory; **c)** the southern limit of present-day Illinois, Indiana, and Ohio; **d)** the western limit of the new United States?

_____

_____

5. Judging from the map on textbook page 215, which nation had the most to lose to the westward expansion of the United States?

_____

6. Where was the Northwest Territory located? (See textbook, page 222.) Label it on your Outline Map.

_____

7. Which present-day states were carved from the Northwest Territory? (See textbook, pages 222–223.)

_____

_____

CHAPTER 10: Outline Map

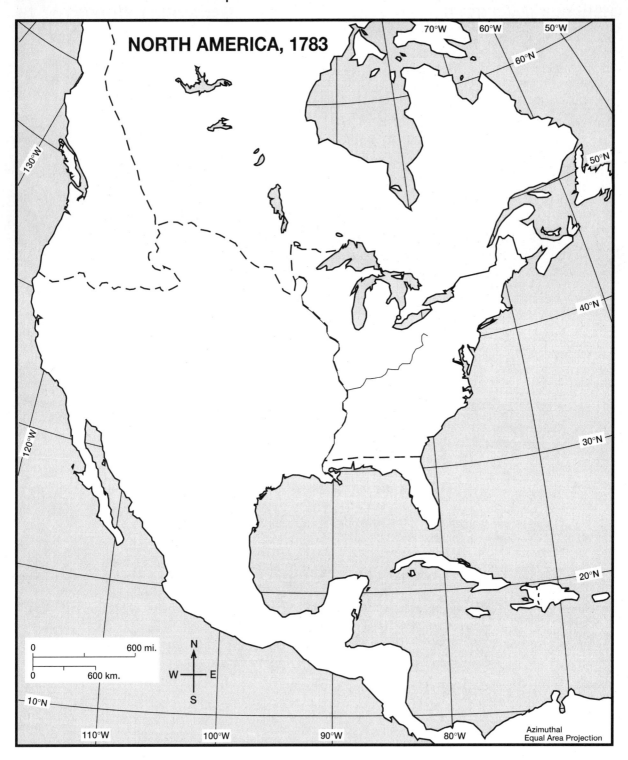

NORTH AMERICA, 1783

Azimuthal
Equal Area Projection

Name _____ Date _____

In the summer of 1781, British General Cornwallis marched his troops northward out of North Carolina and set up camp at Yorktown. While Admiral De Grasse and a French fleet fought off Britain's naval forces at Chesapeake Bay, Generals Washington and Rochambeau led American and French troops southward toward Yorktown. The map below shows the positions of the British and of the Americans and their French allies at Yorktown. Study the map and answer the questions that follow.

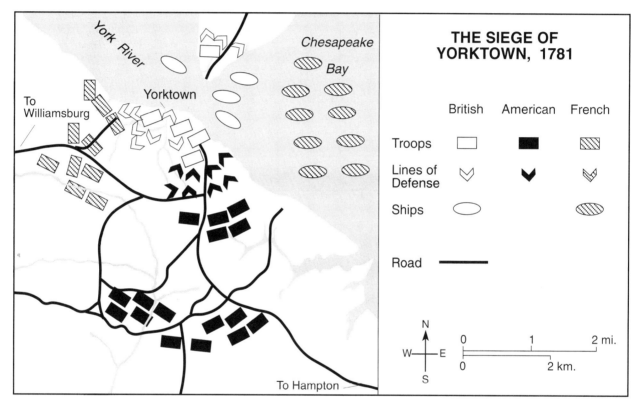

1. What body of water is east of Yorktown? _____

2. What body of water is northwest of Yorktown? _____

3. Why might Cornwallis have chosen Yorktown as a location for his camp? (See textbook, page 213.) _____

_____

_____

4. What prevented Cornwallis from receiving supplies or reinforcements?

_____

5. Who controlled roads leading from Yorktown to the south? _____

_____

6. Who controlled roads leading from Yorktown to the west? _____

7. On October 16, 1781, a storm prevented Cornwallis and his troops from retreating across the York River. Based on the map, how might the weather have influenced Cornwallis's decision to surrender?

_____

_____

_____

8. Geographic Theme: Place   Based on the map above and information in your textbook on pages 212–213, explain how the geography of Yorktown led to the defeat of the British.

_____

_____

_____

_____

_____

_____

_____

_____

Name _____ Date _____

CHAPTER 11   **Map Practice**
The Original Thirteen States   **Geography Worksheet 21**

A. Use the map of United States cities and states on textbook pages
R12–R13 and the map of United States physical features on pages
R14–R15 to locate the following bodies of water and states. Label
these features on the Outline Map on the back of this page.

Bodies of Water   *States*
Atlantic Ocean   Lake Erie   Massachusetts   Delaware
Lake Huron   Ohio River   (2 locations)   Maryland
Lake Ontario   St. Lawrence   New Hampshire   Virginia
Lake Michigan   River   Connecticut   North Carolina
Lake Superior   Chesapeake Bay   New York   South Carolina
                                        Pennsylvania   Georgia
                                        New Jersey

B. Use the Outline Map and the map of United States cities and
states on textbook pages R12–R13 to answer the following questions.

1. The original thirteen states extended from approximately _____ °N to

_____ °N latitude, and from about _____ °W to _____ °W longitude.

2. Use a ruler and the map's scale bar to find the approximate north-south distance of the

original thirteen states. _____

3. At the time of the Constitutional Convention, which New England territory had not yet

become a state? Label this territory on the Outline Map._____

4. Which three natural features help form New York's western boundary? _____

_____

5. What natural feature formed the northwestern boundary of Virginia in 1790?

_____

6. Are most of Pennsylvania's boundaries physical (made by nature) or political (made by

people)? How can you tell? _____

7. Judging by its shape, is the boundary between Georgia and South Carolina a physical or

a political feature? _____

8. In which state did Shays' Rebellion occur? _____

9. In what city was the Constitutional Convention held? Add this city to your outline map.

_____

CHAPTER 11: Outline Map

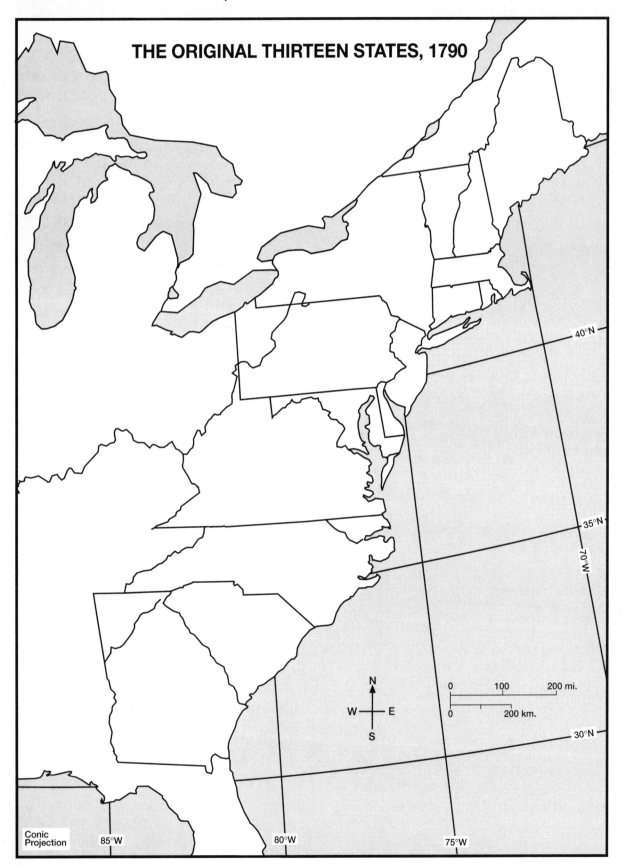

THE ORIGINAL THIRTEEN STATES, 1790

CHAPTER 11
Ratifying the Constitution

Nine of the thirteen states had to agree to the Constitution before it could become law. The map and chart below show the areas that supported and opposed ratification. Study them and answer the questions that follow.

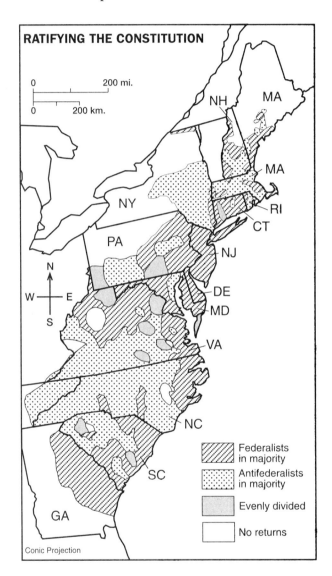

RATIFYING THE CONSTITUTION

0 ___ 200 mi.
0 ___ 200 km.

NH
MA
MA
NY
RI
CT
PA
NJ
N
W—E
S
DE
MD
VA
NC
SC
GA

Federalists in majority
Antifederalists in majority
Evenly divided
No returns

Conic Projection

State	Percentage of Votes For and Against Ratification of the Constitution, by State	
State	**Percentage for**	**Percentage against**
Delaware	100	0
Georgia	100	0
New Jersey	100	0
Maryland	85	15
Connecticut	76	24
North Carolina	72	28
Pennsylvania	67	33
South Carolina	67	33
New Hampshire	55	45
Massachusetts	53	47
New York	53	47
Virginia	53	47
Rhode Island	52	48

1. Which three states supported only the Federalist pro-ratification position?

_____

2. Which position won more support in coastal areas (where the biggest towns were located)?

_____

3. Where was Antifederalist support concentrated? _____

_____

4. The vote in New York was close. From which part of the state did support for ratification come, upstate or downstate?

_____

5. The vote in North Carolina was almost 3 to 1 in favor of ratification. Yet the map shows that Antifederalists were in the majority throughout most of the state. Explain how this could happen.

_____

_____

6. Why is the ratification vote for large areas of Maine (then part of Massachusetts), New York, Pennsylvania, and Georgia not shown on the map?

_____

_____

7. Geographic Theme: Regions What advantage did the Constitution offer to the more populous and prosperous seaboard dwellers? Why might people in rural areas have opposed ratification?

_____

_____

_____

_____

_____

_____

_____

_____

_____

CHAPTER 12
Launching a New Government

Map Practice
Geography Worksheet 23

A. Use the Atlas maps on textbook pages R12–R13 and R14–R15 to locate the following states, cities, and physical features. Label these features on the Outline Map on the back of this page.

Cities		*States*	*Rivers*	*Mountain Ranges*
New York City	Pittsburgh	Maryland	Ohio River	Appalachian
Washington,	New Orleans	Virginia	Mississippi	Mountains
D.C.	Cincinnati	Pennsylvania	River	
Philadelphia		Kentucky		

B. Use the maps on textbook pages R12–R13 and R14–R15 to answer the following questions.

1. Which of the cities listed above lie east of the Appalachian Mountains? _____

    _____

2. Which of the cities listed above are located on the Ohio River? _____

3. Which city is located at 30°N, 90°W? _____

4. What country controlled New Orleans in 1793? Why was this city so important? (See

    textbook, page 302.) _____

    _____

5. The Ohio River forms part of the boundaries of which two states seen on the Outline

    Map? _____

6. In which state did the Whiskey Rebellion take place? (See textbook, pages 303–304.)

    _____

7. To which river did Pinckney's Treaty give American ships access? (See textbook, page

    305.) _____

8. What city became the nation's capital in 1800? _____

CHAPTER 12: Outline Map

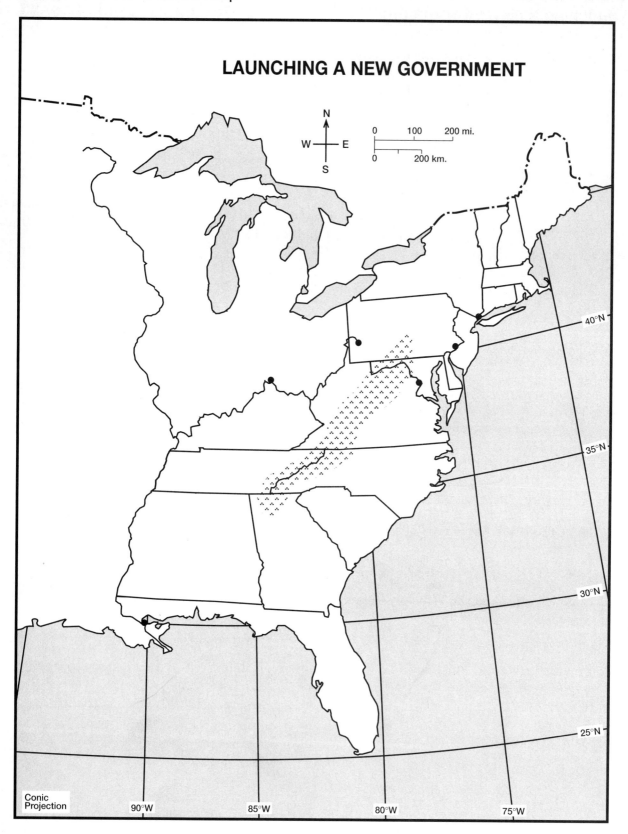

LAUNCHING A NEW GOVERNMENT

N
W E
S

0   100   200 mi.

0   200 km.

40°N

35°N

30°N

25°N

90°W   85°W   80°W   75°W

Conic
Projection

CHAPTER 12
The Nation's Capital

George Washington selected a site on the Potomac River (then spelled "Potomak") for the nation's capital. The original site included land donated by states on both sides of the river, but the boundaries were later changed. The new city was named Washington, D.C., in honor of the first President.

Pierre L'Enfant was chosen to draw up a plan for the city. His plan is below at left. A map showing the location of Washington, D.C., along with its present boundaries, is at right. Study the plan and the map. Then answer the questions that follow.

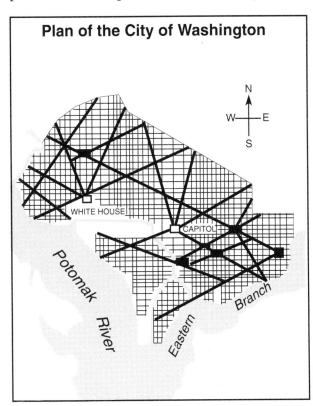

Plan of the City of Washington

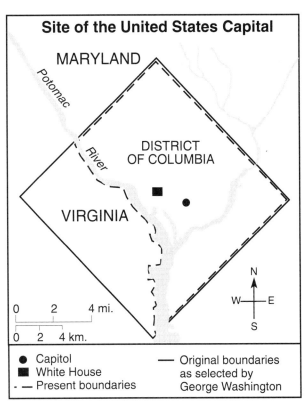

Site of the United States Capital

● Capitol
■ White House
- — Present boundaries

— Original boundaries
  as selected by
  George Washington

1. Which states originally donated lands for the new capital? _____

   _____

2. How have the boundaries of Washington, D.C., changed from Washington's time to

   today? _____

3. On which bank of the Potomac River was the capital built? _____

4. How far is the White House from the Potomac? _____

5. Geographic Theme: Interactions Why, do you think, did L'Enfant plan Washington, D.C., with so many streets meeting at the White House and Capitol?

_____

_____

_____

_____

_____

_____

_____

_____

CHAPTER 13   **Map Practice**
Appalachian Crossings   **Geography Worksheet 25**

A. Use the maps on textbook pages R12–R13 and R14–R15 to locate
the following rivers and states. Label these features on the Outline
Map on the back of this page.

Rivers   *States*
Ohio River   Potomac River   Massachusetts   Maryland
Delaware R.   Hudson River   Connecticut   Virginia
Wabash River   Mohawk River   Rhode Island   North Carolina
Cumberland   Susquehanna   New York   Tennessee
   River   River   Pennsylvania   Kentucky
                                            New Jersey   Delaware

B. Use the map on textbook pages R14–R15 to answer the following
questions.

1. What mountain range appears on the map? _____

2. What difficulties did westward travelers face? (See textbook, page 319.) _____

_____

3. Which river connected the Hudson River with lowlands leading to the great lakes?

_____

4. Which large river flows west from New York state to the Mississippi River?

_____

5. On which river is the United States capital located? _____

6. Describe life on the new frontier. (See textbook, page 319.) _____

_____

_____

_____

7. Why did many westerners favor war with Britain? (See textbook, pages 330–332.)

_____

_____

_____

CHAPTER 13: Outline Map

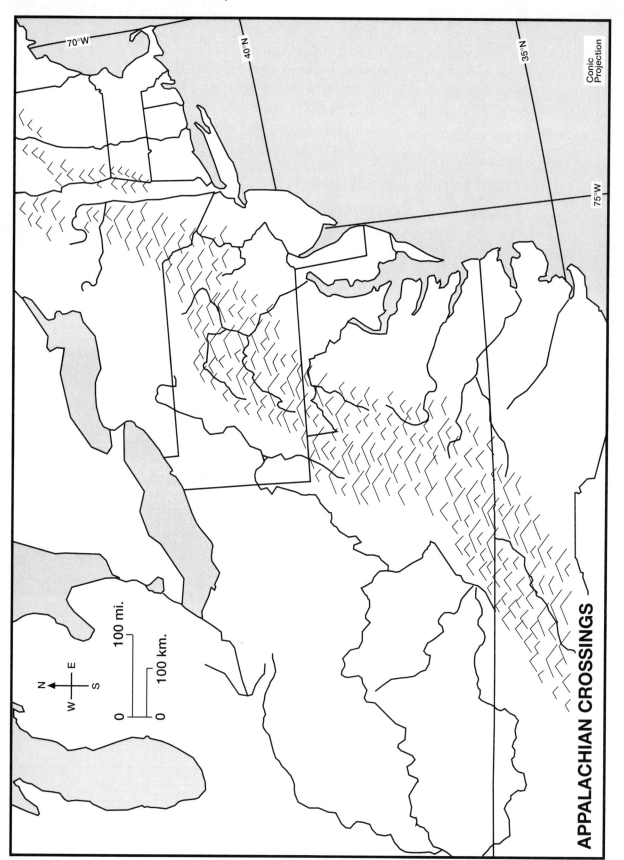

70°W

40°N

35°N

75°W

Conic Projection

100 mi.

100 km.

0

0

N

E

S

W

APPALACHIAN CROSSINGS

Name _____   Date _____

CHAPTER 13
The United States, 1803

In 1802, President Jefferson learned that Spain was planning to turn over the Louisiana Territory to France. One year later, Jefferson offered France about $15 million for the territory and France accepted. Study the map and answer the questions that follow.

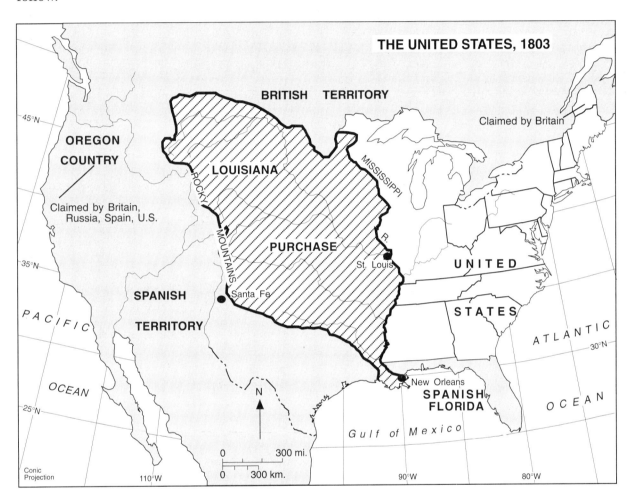

1. What were the approximate latitude and longitude measurements of the United States

   before the Louisiana Purchase? _____

   After? _____

2. About how many times greater was the land area of the United States after the

   Louisiana Purchase than before? _____

3. Which seaport did the United States gain through the purchase? _____

4. What were the eastern and western boundaries of United States after the Louisiana

Purchase? _____

5. The control of which natural feature was the most important geographical advantage of

the purchase? _____

6. Which European nation might have decided to challenge that control? _____

7. What travel routes to the west did the United States gain through the Louisiana

Purchase? _____

8. **Geographic Theme: Regions** With a stroke of his pen, Thomas Jefferson turned the United States into an enormous country. What advantages did such a large land area provide? What risks did it pose?

_____

_____

_____

_____

_____

_____

_____

_____

CHAPTER 14
National Confidence and Economic Expansion

Map Practice
Geography Worksheet 27

A. Use the maps on textbook pages 343, R12–R13, and R14–R15 to locate the following states, cities, bodies of water, and mountain ranges. Label these features on the Outline Map on the back of this page.

States		*Cities*	*Bodies of Water*	*Mountain Ranges*
Maryland	Virginia	New York City	Atlantic Ocean	Appalachian
Ohio	Rhode Island	Boston	Ohio River	Mountains
Indiana	Massachusetts	Albany	Lake Erie	
Illinois	Georgia	Buffalo	Hudson River	
Michigan	South Carolina	New Orleans	Mississippi	
Mississippi	Louisiana	Philadelphia	River	
Alabama	Kentucky		Gulf of Mexico	
Florida			Erie Canal	

B. Use the map on textbook page 343 to answer the following questions.

1. Which cities were connected by the Miami and Erie Canal? _____

2. How long was the Erie Canal? (See textbook, page 344.) _____

3. How many canals on the map ran generally north to south? _____

4. Which canals would a Waltham textile manufacturer use to get his cloth to Evansville?

_____

5. Which canal helped link Chicago with the Mississippi River? _____

6. Which canal ran through Indiana? _____

7. Which canals crossed the Appalachian Mountains? _____

8. Which canal opened the upper Ohio Valley and the Great Lakes region to settlement?

(See textbook, pages 344–345.) _____

9. Which state had more than two canals running through it? Name the canals. _____

_____

10. What rivers were linked by the Pennsylvania Canal? _____

11. Describe one way a Mississippi farmer could get his crop to Cleveland by an all-water

route. _____

CHAPTER 14: Outline Map

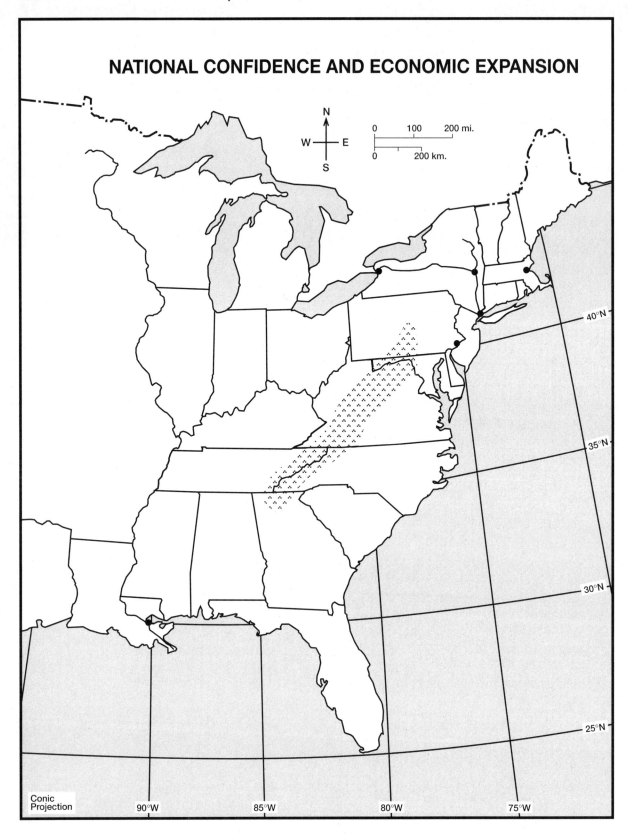

NATIONAL CONFIDENCE AND ECONOMIC EXPANSION

N
W — E
S

0   100   200 mi.

0   200 km.

40°N

35°N

30°N

25°N

90°W   85°W   80°W   75°W

Conic
Projection

CHAPTER 14
King Cotton

"Cotton is King!" was a familiar phrase in the Old South. Indeed, the crop controlled the economy of the region with the power of a monarch. Cotton cultivation shaped the lives of many southerners, from white plantation-owning families to the black slaves who worked the fields. Study the maps below and answer the questions that follow.

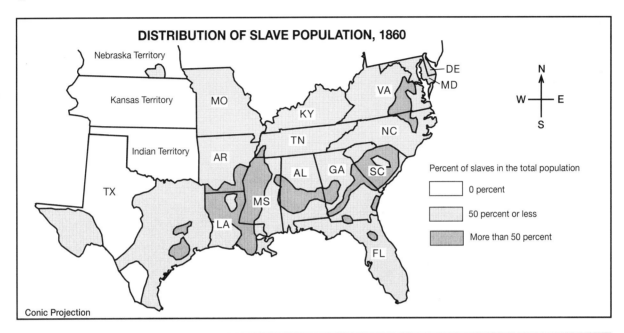

DISTRIBUTION OF SLAVE POPULATION, 1860

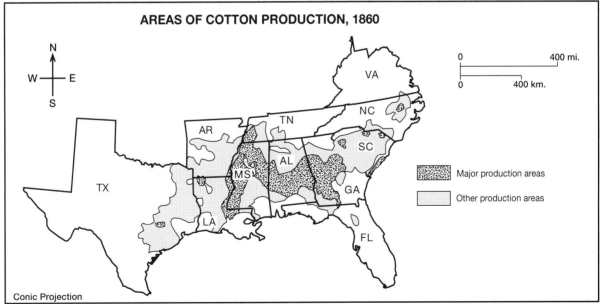

AREAS OF COTTON PRODUCTION, 1860

1. In which region of Texas was cotton produced? _____

2. How far north was cotton grown in 1860? _____

3. Outside of Virginia, which five southern states had the largest areas in which slaves made up more than 50 percent of the population?

_____

4. In which territory were some slaves held? _____

5. Judging from the map, were slaves involved in other parts of the economy of the South

besides cotton? Explain. _____

_____

6. Geographic Theme: Interactions What was the relationship between cotton production and the density of the slave population in 1860?

_____

_____

_____

_____

_____

_____

_____

_____

Name _____ Date _____

A. Use the maps on textbook pages 366 and 371 to locate the following states and Indian nations. Label these on the Outline Map on the back of this page.

States and
  Territories   New York   Illinois   *Indian Nations*
Missouri   Virginia   Florida Terr.   Cherokee
Maine   Georgia   Arkansas Terr.   Sauk and Fox
Tennessee   Kentucky   South Carolina   Seminole
Ohio   Michigan Terr. Massachusetts

B. Use the maps on textbook pages 366 and 371 to answer the following questions.

1. Where was the Missouri Compromise line drawn? _____

   How did it attempt to maintain the balance of power in Congress? _____

   _____

2. Which slave states and territories were located north of the Missouri Compromise line?

   _____

3. Which free states and territories lay west of the Mississippi River in 1820? _____

   _____

4. Which territories were open to slavery in 1820? _____

5. What route did the Seminole Indians take in their forced move to the Indian Territory?

   _____

   _____

6. How long was the Trail of Tears? _____

7. Through what states did the Cherokee pass during their forced march to the Indian

   Territory? _____

   _____

8. Why was the Missouri Compromise only a temporary solution? _____

   _____

CHAPTER 15: Outline Map

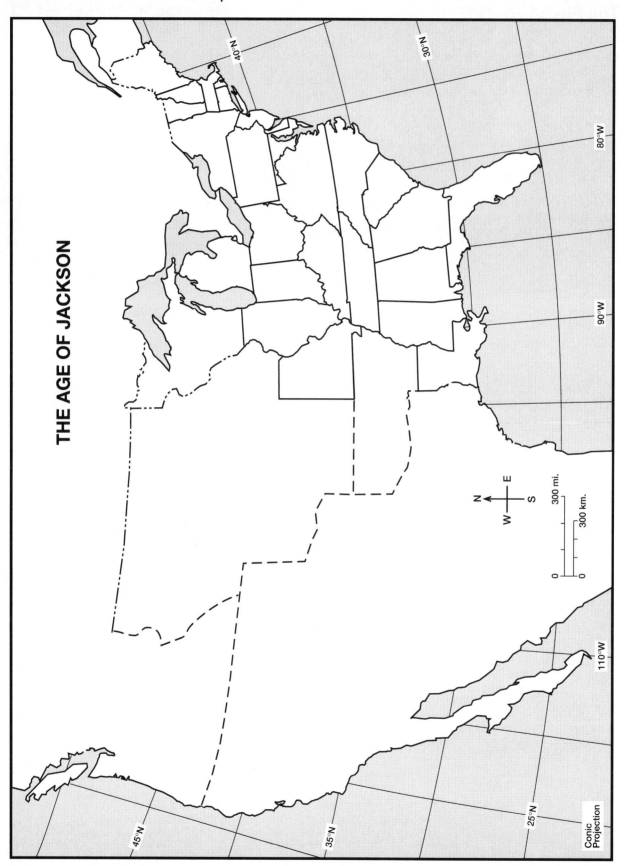

THE AGE OF JACKSON

40°N

30°N

80°W

90°W

110°W

45°N

35°N

25°N

N
E
W ——→
S

300 mi.

300 km.

0

0

Conic Projection

Name _____ Date _____

In 1828 Andrew Jackson waged his second battle for the presidency against the incumbent, John Quincy Adams. Four years earlier, Jackson had won 99 electoral votes to Adams's 84 but did not win a majority. William Crawford and Henry Clay, the two other candidates running for President, won the remaining 76 electoral votes. The outcome of that presidential race was determined by the House of Representatives. The members of the House chose Adams to be President, and Jackson was forced to wait until 1828 to try again.

The map below shows how each state voted in the election of 1828. Study the map and then answer the questions that follow.

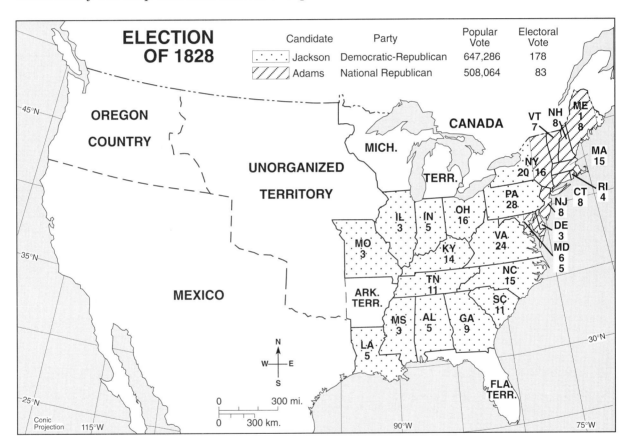

Candidate	Party	Popular Vote	Electoral Vote
Jackson	Democratic-Republican	647,286	178
Adams	National Republican	508,064	83

1. Which states cast their electoral votes for both candidates? _____

2. How many more popular votes did Jackson receive than Adams? _____

3. How many more electoral votes did Jackson receive in 1828 than in 1824? _____

4. Which two states had the largest number of electoral votes? In which region were these

states located? _____

5. Where was support for Adams the strongest? In which regions of the country was

support for Jackson the strongest? _____

_____

_____

6. How many electoral votes did the slave states have? Was this a majority of the electoral

votes? (See the map on textbook page 366.) _____

7. Geographic Theme: Movement What effect did the western movement of the population have on national politics? Why?

_____

_____

_____

_____

_____

_____

_____

_____

CHAPTER 16   **Map Practice**
Immigration in the Mid-1800s   **Geography Worksheet 31**

A. Use the maps on textbook pages 386 and R12–R13 to locate the
following states and cities. Label them on the Outline Map on the
back of this page.

States   *Cities*
Ohio   Missouri   Maine   San Francisco   Baltimore
Indiana   Texas   New York   San Antonio   Washington,
Illinois   Minnesota   Maryland   New York   D.C.
Iowa   Kentucky   South Carolina   Boston
Kentucky   Massachusetts   Philadelphia
Wisconsin   Georgia

B. Use the map on textbook page 386 to answer the following questions.

1. In which states on the map was the percentage of German immigrants at least 8 per-

    cent of the population? _____

    _____

2. In which cities would you find more than 10,000 Irish immigrants? _____

    _____

3. In which states did German immigrants make up from 2 to 3 percent of the population?

    _____

    _____

4. In which region of the country did German and Irish immigrants make up the smallest

    percentages of state population? _____

5. What percentage of Maine's population was German? Irish? _____

6. How were German patterns of settlement different from those of the Irish? _____

    _____

7. Explain the "push–pull" of immigration. _____

    _____

    _____

    _____

CHAPTER 16: Outline Map

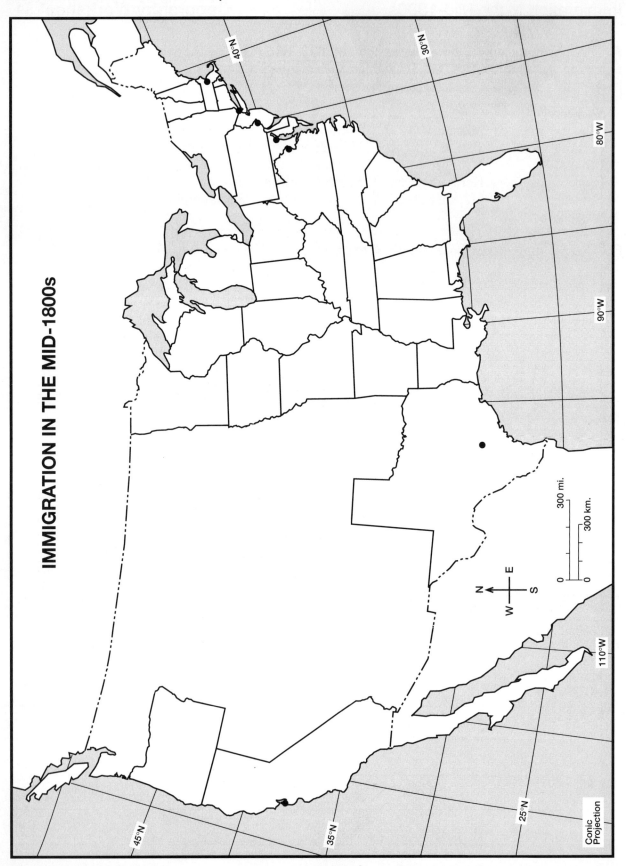

IMMIGRATION IN THE MID-1800s

300 mi.

300 km.

N
W E
S

Conic Projection

CHAPTER 16
The Underground Railroad

When runaway slaves reached the North, their dangerous jour-
ney and troubles were not over. A runaway who was caught in a
free state could be sent back to bondage in the South. As a
result, runaway slaves needed to find shelter in the North. They
found this shelter at the "stations" of the Underground Railroad.
Some stations were in major cities, while others were in small
towns.

   The map below shows some routes and stations of the
Underground Railroad in the North. Study it and answer the
questions that follow.

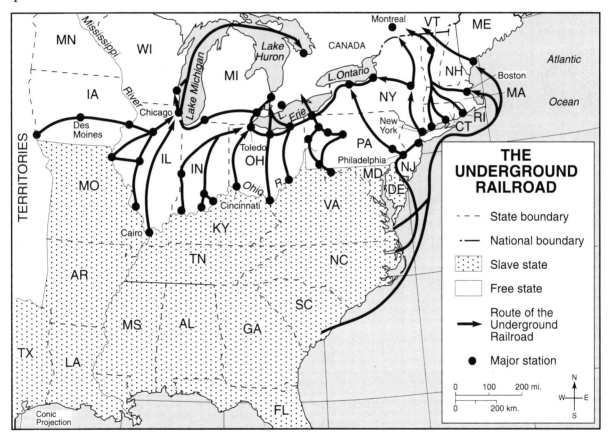

1. Where did all the routes on this map eventually lead? _____

2. Using the map's scale bar, determine about how far a slave reaching Cairo, Illinois,
   would have to travel to reach Chicago.

   _____

3. Once escaped slaves reached Chicago, what route would they take from there to

   freedom? _____

4. How could slaves living near the Atlantic coast avoid the dangers of traveling through

the South? _____

_____

5. Look at the map on textbook pages 396–397. In addition to Canada, where else did

runaway slaves go? _____

_____

6. Why did runaway slaves avoid Indian Territory? (See textbook, page 396.)

_____

7. Geographic Theme: Location From which states do you think it would have been
hardest to escape? Explain your answer.

_____

_____

_____

_____

_____

_____

_____

_____

CHAPTER 17
Trails Across the West

A. Use the maps on textbook pages 417 and R14–R15 to locate the following features. Label them on the Outline Map on the back of this page.

Bodies of Water	*Landforms*	*Cities*	*Trails*	*Other Features*
Mississippi R.	Great Plains	Independence	Oregon Trail	Oregon
Platte R.	Rocky	Santa Fe	California Trail	Country
Missouri R.	Mountains	Fort Vancouver	South Pass	Mexico
Columbia R.	Great Basin	St. Louis		Canada
Rio Grande		San Francisco		
Gila R.		Salt Lake City		
Great Salt				
Lake				
Pacific Ocean				

B. Use the map on textbook page 417 to answer the following questions.

1. Which two trails began in Independence, Missouri? Where did each end? _____

_____

2. How might travelers from the East have arrived in Independence? _____

_____

3. Which trail ended in Salt Lake City? Where did this trail begin? _____

4. Which trail followed three rivers? Which rivers were they? _____

_____

5. Which city was an end point for one trail and the starting point for another? Which

   trails were they? _____

6. Which trail led to Sacramento? Where did this trail originate? _____

_____

7. Which trail was the longest? _____

8. How does the map suggest that Bent's Fort was an important trading post at this time?

_____

9. How do you think the Old Spanish Trail got its name? _____

_____

CHAPTER 17: Outline Map

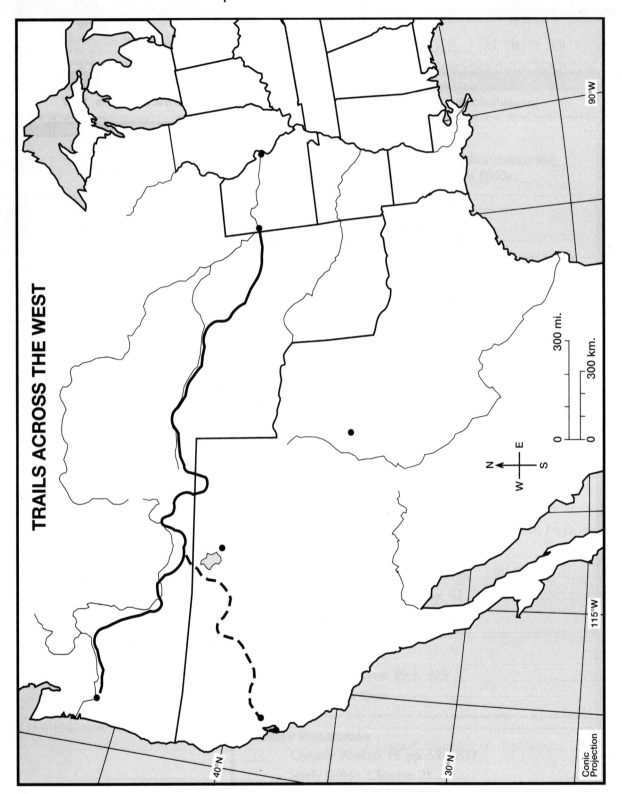

Name _____ Date _____

Between 1845 and 1853 the United States gained more than a
million square miles of land from Mexico. That land became part
of 10 states in the present–day United States. The map below
shows the land acquired from Mexico, the states formed from
that land, and the dates they achieved statehood. Study the map
and answer the questions that follow.

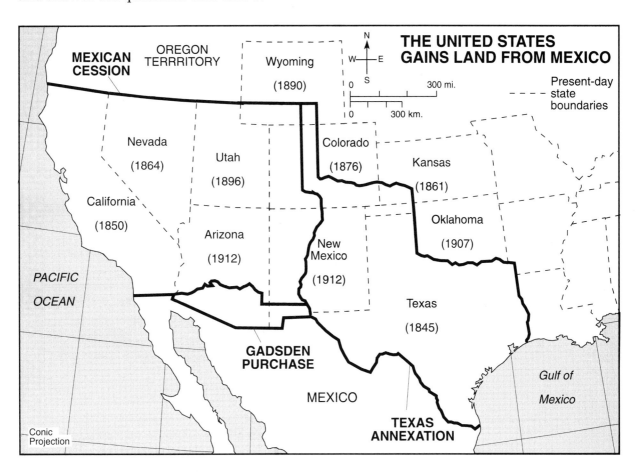

1. Which states acquired all of their land from the Mexican Cession? _____

_____

2. Which state acquired part of its land from the Mexican Cession, part of its land from the
   Gadsden Purchase, and part of its land from the Texas Annexation?

_____

3. Which is the westernmost state in the Gadsden Purchase? _____

4. Which state in the Texas Annexation was the first to achieve statehood? _____

5. In what year did Colorado become a state? _____

6. How many states acquired land from the Texas annexation? _____

7. Geographic Theme: Interactions Statehood came early for some of the lands gained from Mexico, such as California and Texas. For other lands, however, statehood did not come until the twentieth century. What might account for the difference in the dates of statehood for these lands?

_____

_____

_____

_____

_____

_____

_____

_____

CHAPTER 18
Steps to Civil War

A. Use the maps on textbook pages 442, 449, R12–R13, and
R14–R15 to locate the following features. Label these features on the
Outline Map on the back of this page.

States		*Cities and Forts*	*Water Areas*
Virginia	Maine	Harpers Ferry	Mississippi River
Kansas	Tennessee	Chicago	Ohio River
South Carolina	Texas	Fort Sumter	Great Lakes
Missouri	Illinois		
Kentucky	Nebraska		

B. Use the maps on textbook pages 442 and 449 to answer the following questions.

1. Which state was admitted to the Union as a slave state as part of the Missouri

   Compromise in 1820? _____

2. How many slave states were there in 1820? _____

3. Where was the Missouri Compromise line drawn? _____

4. Which western state was admitted to the Union as part of the Compromise of 1850? Was

   it admitted as a slave or free state? _____

5. How was the question of slavery in Utah Territory and New Mexico Territory handled in

   the Compromise of 1850? Explain. (See textbook, page 440.) _____

   _____

   _____

6. Which states voted for Bell in the election of 1860? _____

7. How many states did Lincoln carry in the election of 1860? _____

   Did Lincoln win a majority of the popular vote? (See textbook, page 449.) _____

8. Which state was the first to secede from the Union? (See textbook, page 449.)

   _____

CHAPTER 18: Outline Map

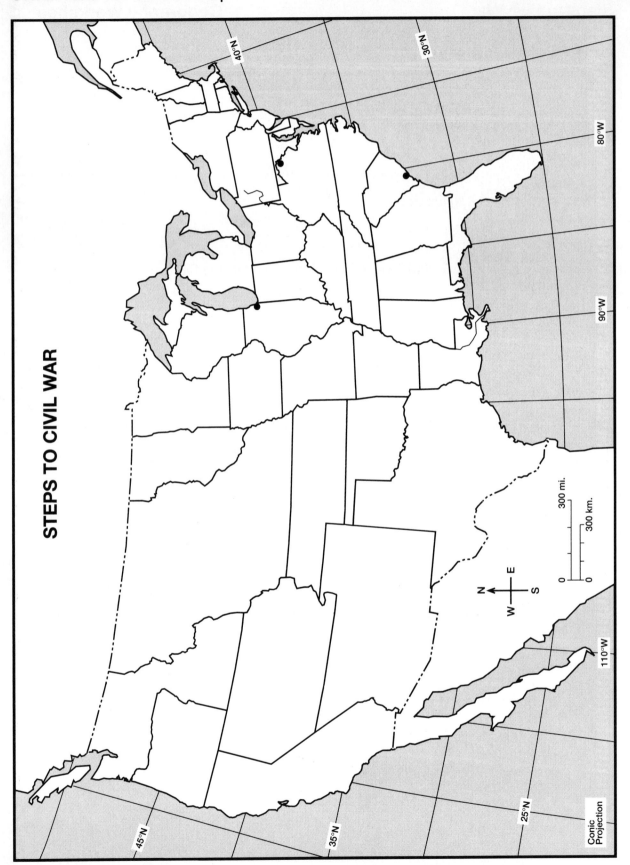

STEPS TO CIVIL WAR

CHAPTER 18
Fort Sumter Falls

After South Carolina seceded from the Union, President Lincoln sent supplies to Fort Sumter—a Union fort located in a harbor along the Carolina coast. In the early morning of April 12, 1861, Confederate troops attacked Fort Sumter. Soon after, the Union supply ships arrived but did not attempt to reach the fort. Study the map below and answer the questions that follow.

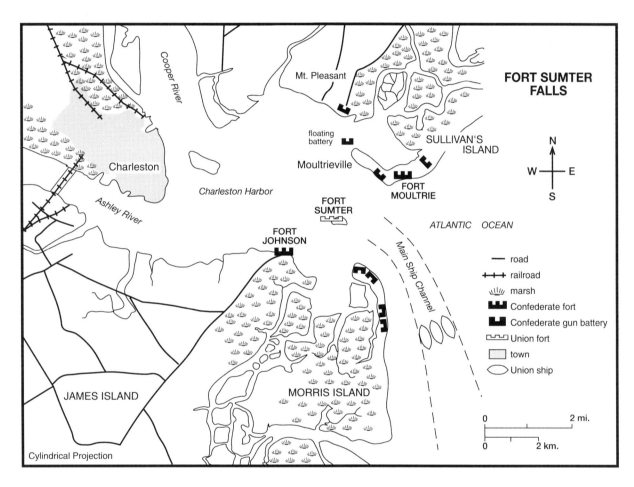

1. On what type of landform was Fort Sumter located? _____

2. Which city and harbor lay near the fort? _____

3. Which two rivers empty into the harbor? _____

4. How many Confederate forts were located in the harbor? What were their names?

_____

5. What other defenses did the Confederates have? Describe these. (Use a dictionary, if

necessary.) _____

_____

6. Confederate General Beauregard said he would form a "circle of fire" around Fort

Sumter. What did he mean by this? _____

_____

7. Which passage did the Union ships have to use to reach the fort? _____

8. If the Union ships had been warships, could Union soldiers have landed on Morris
Island and Sullivan's Island and approached the Confederate defenses from the rear?
What physical features shown on the map might have hindered them? Why?

_____

9. Geographic Theme: Location The Union ships did not attempt to reach the fort, and
it fell to the Confederacy. What made Fort Sumter so easy to isolate? What would have
happened if the Union supply ships had attempted to get through?

_____

_____

_____

_____

_____

_____

_____

_____

CHAPTER 19
The Civil War

A. Use the maps on textbook pages 463 and 477 to locate the following battle sites, cities, states, and bodies of water. Label these features on the Outline Map on the back of this page.

Battle Sites	*Cities*	*States*		*Bodies of Water*
Ft. Sumter	Washington,	Virginia	Texas	Mississippi
Ft. Henry	D.C.	Maryland	Kentucky	River
Ft. Donelson	Richmond	North Carolina	South Carolina	Ohio River
Gettysburg	Cairo	Tennessee	Mississippi	Atlantic Ocean
Vicksburg	Nashville	Arkansas	Louisiana	Gulf of Mexico
Pea Ridge	New Orleans	Alabama	Illinois	
Shiloh				
New Orleans				

B. Use the maps on textbook pages 463 and 477 to answer the following questions.

1. Which side won the Battle of Chancellorsville? _____

2. Who commanded the Confederate forces at the Battle of Gettysburg? Who commanded

   the Union forces? _____

3. Which Confederate states did not have areas controlled or won by the Union between

   1863 and 1865? _____

4. Which parts of Florida fell under Union control between 1863 and 1865? _____

   _____

5. Approximately how long did it take Grant to advance to Chattanooga after his victory at

   Vicksburg? How far had he traveled? _____

6. Which parts of the Confederacy were blockaded by the Union? _____

   _____

7. Which battle was fought at approximately 35°N, 85°W? _____

8. What states did Lee travel through in his march from Chancellorsville to Gettysburg?

   _____

   _____

9. What states did Sherman travel through in his march from Atlanta to Raleigh?

   _____

CHAPTER 19: Outline Map

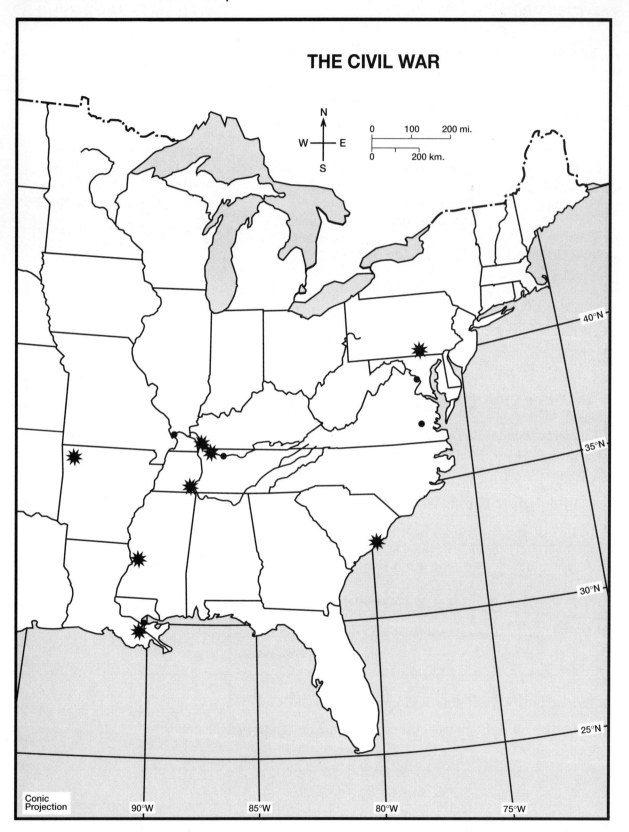

THE CIVIL WAR

N
W — E
S

0   100   200 mi.
0   200 km.

40°N
35°N
30°N
25°N

90°W   85°W   80°W   75°W

Conic
Projection

CHAPTER 19
Railroads and the Civil War

Railroads played an important part in the Civil War. They provided the quickest and easiest way to move troops and supplies.
When the Civil War began, the United States had about 30,625
miles (49,276 kilometers) of railroad track, as shown on the map
below. Study the map and answer the questions that follow.

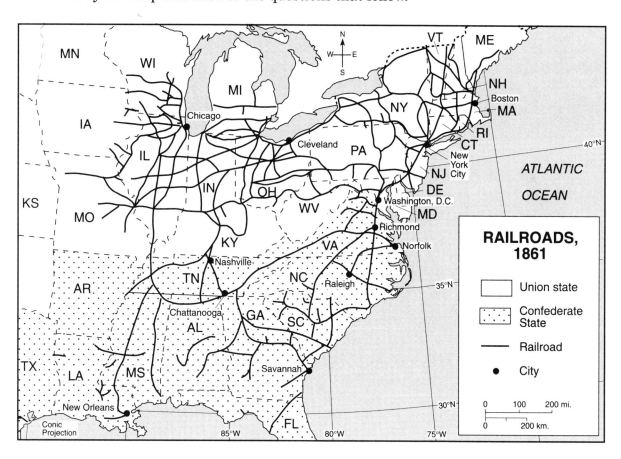

1. Which region had more railroad track in 1861, the North or the South? _____

2. If the Confederacy wanted to ship supplies from Raleigh to Nashville, what railroad

   routes would the supplies take? _____

   _____

   _____

   _____

3. How long was the railroad trip from Raleigh to Nashville? What is the distance between

   these two cities in a straight line? _____

4. **Geographic Theme: Regions** In what ways was the South's railroad network weak? How would this hurt the South during the Civil War?

_____

_____

_____

_____

_____

_____

_____

_____

CHAPTER 20
The Election of 1876

A. Use the Atlas map on textbook pages R12–R13 to locate the following states. Label these features on the Outline Map on the back of this page.

States

Massachusetts	New Hampshire	Indiana	Pennsylvania
New York	North Carolina	Ohio	Virginia
Ohio	South Carolina	Arkansas	West Virginia
California	Maine	Alabama	Delaware
Texas	Nevada	Georgia	Maryland
Kansas	Oregon	Louisiana	Kentucky
Florida	Minnesota	Tennessee	Michigan
Maryland	Illinois	Vermont	Missouri
Connecticut	Nebraska		Colorado
Rhode Island	Iowa		

B. Use the Outline Map to answer the following questions.

1. How many electoral votes did Massachusetts have? _____

2. How many states clearly supported Tilden? _____ Hayes? _____

3. Who won more undisputed electoral votes? _____

4. Which states had disputed results? _____

5. Which candidate became President? (See textbook, page 494.) _____

6. Which candidate did most southern states support? _____

7. Why might Tilden and his supporters have been angered by the final results of the election? Explain. _____

_____

_____

_____

_____

CHAPTER 20: Outline Map

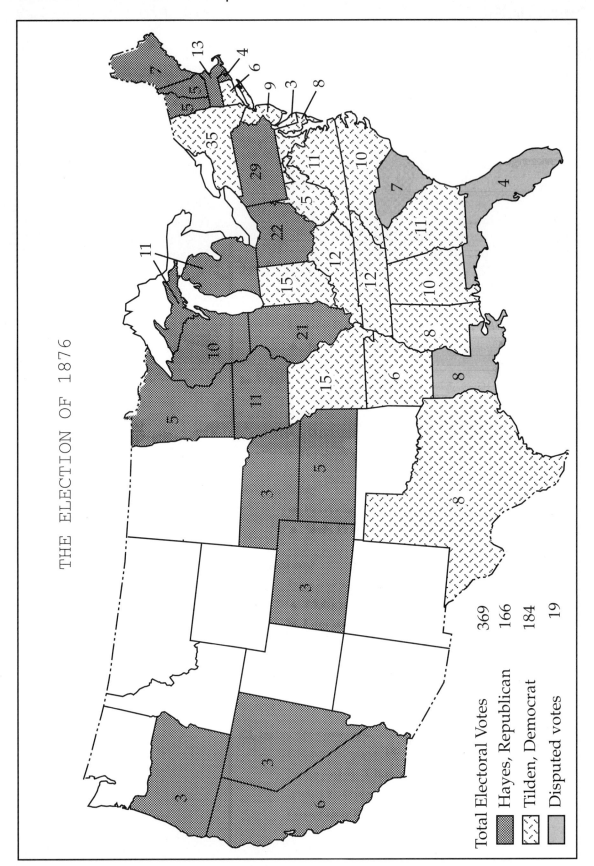

THE ELECTION OF 1876

Total Electoral Votes	369
Hayes, Republican	166
Tilden, Democrat	184
Disputed votes	19

Name _____ Date _____

The industries involved in warfare and the destruction that war causes have important economic effects. The Civil War altered the economic map of the United States. Study the maps below and answer the questions.

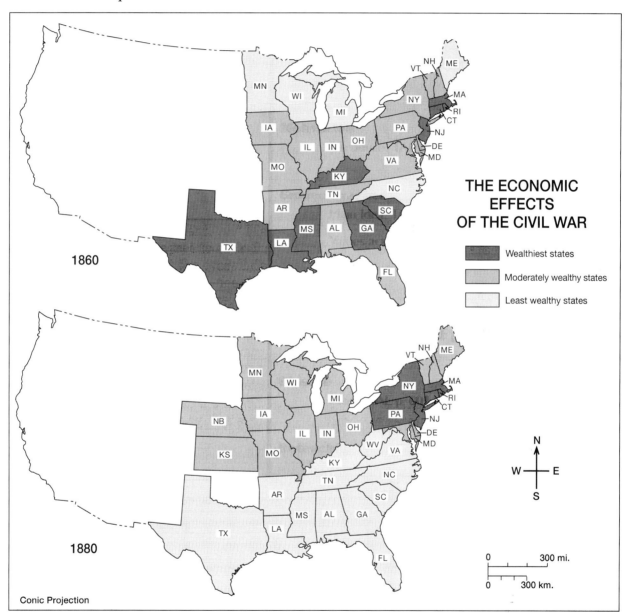

THE ECONOMIC
EFFECTS
OF THE CIVIL WAR

Wealthiest states

Moderately wealthy states

Least wealthy states

1860

1880

Conic Projection

0   300 mi.
0   300 km.

1. In which region were most of the richest states located in 1880? _____

2. Which Confederate states were among the wealthiest states before the Civil War? On

what was their economic wealth based? _____

_____

3. Which of these Confederate states were among the least wealthy by 1880?

_____

4. Which northern states were among the richest states before the Civil War? Compare

their economic positions after the war. _____

_____

_____

_____

5. Which border state ranked among the richest ten before the Civil War? _____

6. Which states on this map were formed between 1860 and 1880? _____

_____

7. Which region had the larger share of the wealthiest states before the Civil War?

_____

8. Describe the position of the Confederate states before and after the Civil War.

_____

_____

9. Geographic Theme: Regions At the end of the Civil War, one region was much richer
than it had been and one region was much poorer. What geographic and social factors
contributed to the shift in wealth for both the North and South?

_____

_____

_____

_____

_____

_____

_____

CHAPTER 21
Railroads in 1900

A. Use the map on textbook page 507 to locate the following bodies of water, cities, and railroad lines. Label these features on the Outline Map on the back of this page.

Bodies of Water	*Cities and Towns*		*Railroads*
Atlantic Ocean	Atlanta	El Paso	Central Pacific
Pacific Ocean	New York City	Cheyenne	Union Pacific
Lake Superior	Washington, D.C.	New Orleans	Pennsylvania
Lake Michigan	Pittsburgh	Santa Fe	Illinois Central
Lake Huron	Chicago	San Francisco	Great Northern
Lake Ontario	Omaha	Promontory	New York
Lake Erie	Dallas	Los Angeles	Central
	Fargo	Seattle	Southern Pacific
			Texas & Pacific

B. Use the map on textbook page 507 to answer the following questions.

1. What railroad lines carried passengers from New York City to Chicago? _____

_____

2. What two railroad lines met at Promontory, Utah, to form the first transcontinental

railroad? _____

3. What city was located at the eastern end of the first transcontinental railroad?

_____ At the western end? _____

4. Through how many time zones would a passenger going from Pittsburgh to Cheyenne

travel? _____

5. If it is 2:00 P.M. in New Orleans, what time is it in each of the following cities?

   a. Dallas _____

   b. Denver _____

   c. Pittsburgh _____

6. Which city lay at the intersection of several major railroad lines? _____

7. Use the scale bar to determine about how many miles a train ride from Chicago to

Omaha covered. _____

CHAPTER 21: Outline Map

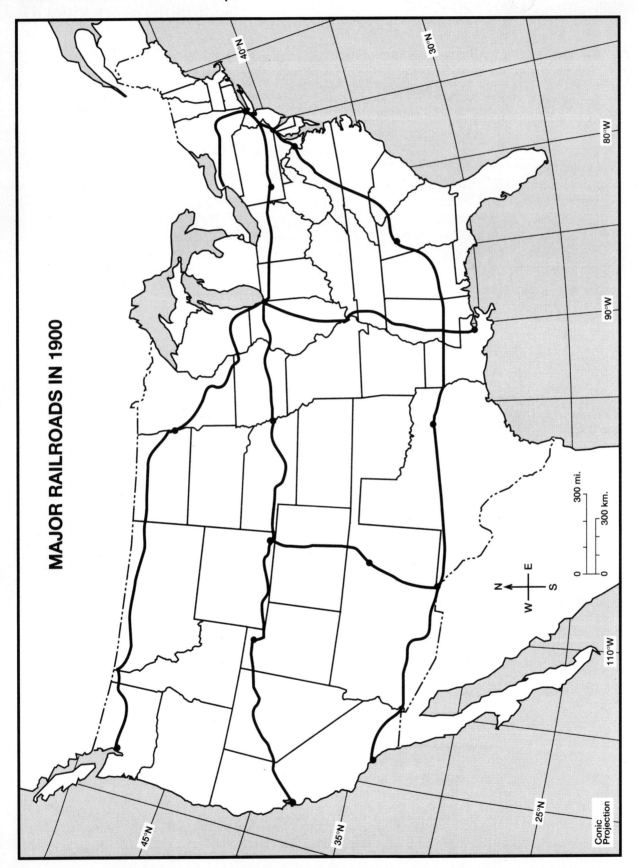

MAJOR RAILROADS IN 1900

40°N

30°N

80°W

90°W

110°W

25°N

45°N

35°N

Conic
Projection

300 mi.

300 km.

N
W — E
S

Name _____ Date _____

In the late nineteenth century, conflicts between workers and
owners led to many work stoppages or strikes. Among the major
issues were wages, hours, and the right to unionize. The graphs
below show information about work stoppages between 1890 and
1895. Answer the questions that follow.

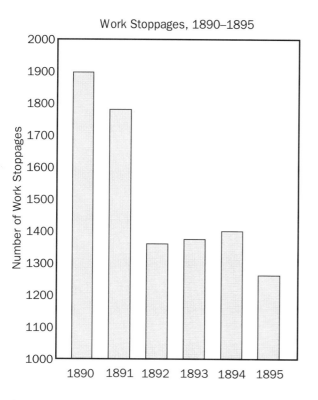

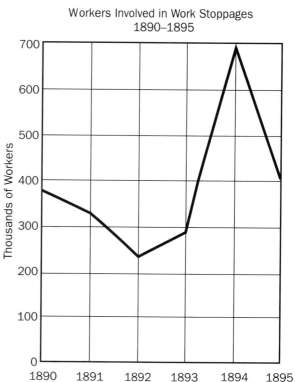

1. About how many work stoppages took place in 1895? _____

2. In which year shown on the bar graph did the most work stoppages take place?

   _____

3. About how many workers were involved in work stoppages in 1893? _____

   In 1895? _____

4. In which year shown on the line graph were the most workers involved in work

   stoppages? _____

5. What major strike took place in each of the following years? (See textbook pages 519–525.)

   a. 1877 _____

   b. 1892 _____

   c. 1894 _____

6. In the year of the Pullman Strike how did the number of workers involved in work stoppages differ from the previous year?

   _____

7. **Geographic Theme: Movement** What effect do you think railroad strikes might have had on the economy during the late 1800s? Do you think strikes were an effective way for workers to protest? Explain. (See textbook, pages 519–525.)

   _____

   _____

   _____

   _____

   _____

   _____

   _____

   _____

   _____

CHAPTER 22   **Map Practice**
Growth of Cities in the Great Lakes Region   **Geography Worksheet 43**

A. Use the maps on textbook pages 541, 544–545, and R12–R13 to locate the following cities, states, and bodies of water. Label these features on the Outline Map on the back of this page.

States		*Cities*		*Bodies of Water*
New York	Michigan	Buffalo	Detroit	Lake Ontario
Pennsylvania	Wisconsin	Pittsburgh	Chicago	Lake Erie
Ohio	Minnesota	Cleveland	Milwaukee	Lake Huron
Indiana	Iowa	Columbus	St. Louis	Lake Michigan
Illinois	Missouri	Toledo	Minneapolis	Ohio R.
		Cincinnati		Mississippi R.

B. Use the map on textbook pages 544–545 to answer the following questions.

1. Which Great Lakes port is located at the southern end of Lake Michigan? _____

   At the eastern end of Lake Erie? _____

2. Which states are shown as having sawmill centers? _____

3. Which industry aided the growth of Pittsburgh, Cleveland, and Chicago? _____

   _____

4. What river was used to transport goods from Minneapolis to St. Louis? _____

5. Name three ways that goods might have been transported between Buffalo and Toledo.

   _____

   _____

6. How might goods have been transported between Columbus and Indianapolis?

   _____

7. What advantage did cities located on the Great Lakes have over other cities in this

   region? _____

   _____

8. Based on information from this map, how did transportation help Chicago become the

   Midwest's largest city? _____

   _____

   _____

CHAPTER 22: Outline Map

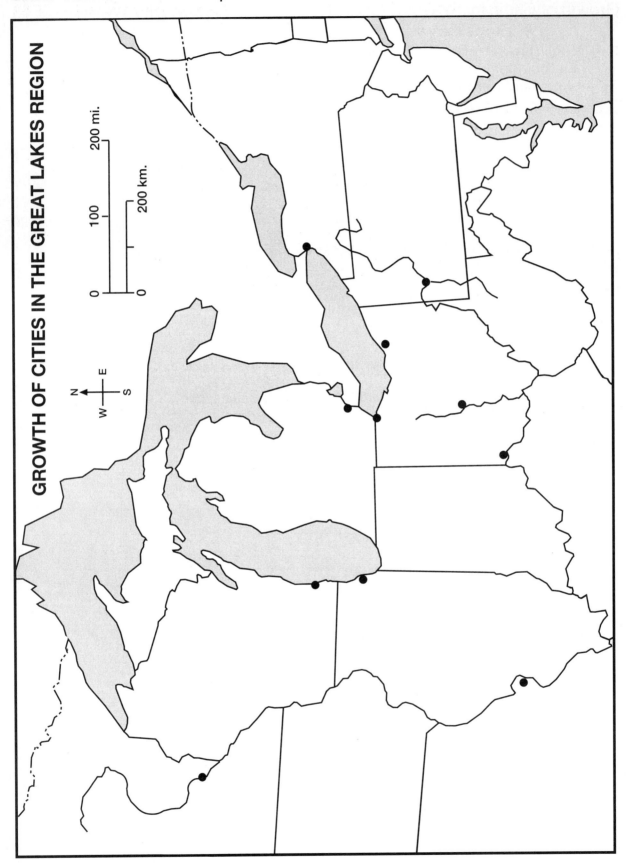

GROWTH OF CITIES IN THE GREAT LAKES REGION

200 mi.

100

200 km.

0

0

N
W E
S

Name _____   Date _____

CHAPTER 22
Immigration, 1820–1920

Immigration from Europe in the 1800s and early 1900s resulted
in rapid urban growth in the United States. The map below
shows the nations from which European immigrants came. The
pie graphs show how immigration changed over time. Study
them and answer the questions that follow.

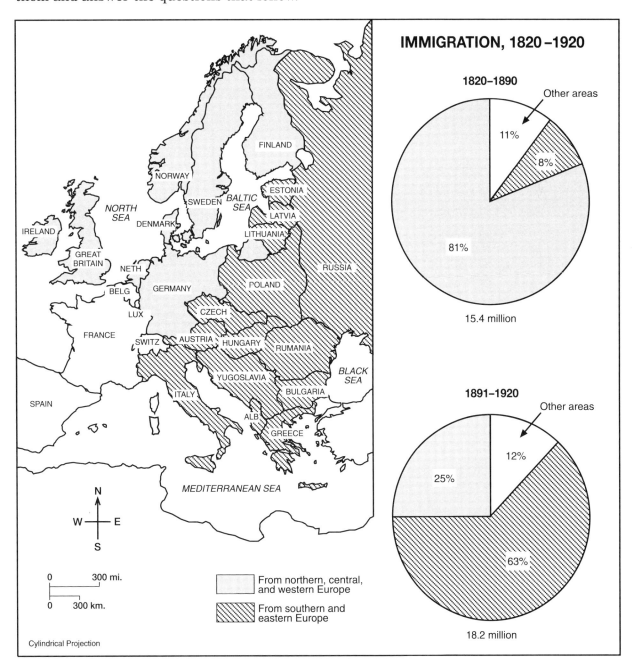

1. How many immigrants arrived in America between 1820 and 1920? _____

2. Did more immigrants arrive in 1820–1890 or 1891–1920? _____

3. Before 1890, from which regions of Europe did most immigrants come to the United

States? _____

4. What percentage of immigrants who came before 1890 came from southern and eastern

Europe? _____ What percentage of immigrants came from these regions

of Europe after 1890? _____

5. Relatively few immigrants from 1820–1920 came from France or Spain. How are these

countries shown on the map? _____

6. What percentage of immigrants who came before 1890 came from northern, central, and

western Europe? _____ What percentage of immigrants came from these

parts of Europe after 1890? _____

7. Geographic Theme: Movement Explain how immigration to the United States
changed after 1890. Discuss reasons why immigrants settled in American cities in the
late 1800s. (See textbook, pages 529–533.)

_____

_____

_____

_____

_____

_____

CHAPTER 23
Cattle Trails and Cow Towns

A. Use the map on textbook page 567 to locate the following cities, states and territories, and cattle trails. Label these features on the Outline Map on the back of this page.

Cities		*States and Territories*	*Cattle Trails*
Abilene	Kansas City	New Mexico	Shawnee Trail
Dodge City	Ogallala	Texas	Chisholm Trail
Chicago	Cheyenne	Kansas	Western Trail
St. Louis	San Antonio	Missouri	Goodnight-
Omaha	Wichita	Nebraska	Loving Trail
Denver	Topeka	Illinois	
Pueblo			

B. Use the map on textbook page 567 to answer the following questions.

1. What was the purpose of the cattle trails? (See textbook, pages 567–568.) _____

   _____

   _____

   _____

2. Near what city did the Chisholm and Shawnee Trails start? _____

3. Which cattle trail extended farthest west? _____

4. Which cow towns were shipping points along the Western Trail? _____

   _____

5. Which cattle trails ended at railheads on the Union Pacific Road? _____

   _____

6. Which cow towns were shipping points from which cattle were sent to packing houses in

   Chicago? _____

7. Use the scale bar to determine the distance of the long drive along the Chisholm Trail

   from San Antonio to Abilene. _____

CHAPTER 23: Outline Map

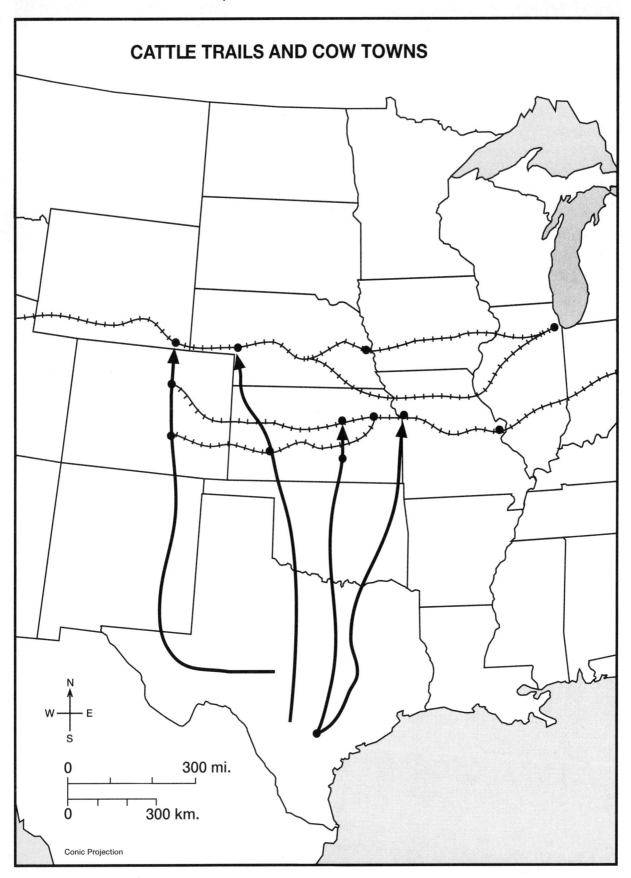

CATTLE TRAILS AND COW TOWNS

0   300 mi.

0   300 km.

Conic Projection

CHAPTER 23
Land Regions of the West

The western United States contains many land regions. Each region has its distinctive landforms and climate. The map below shows land regions and physical features of the American West. Study the map and answer the questions that follow.

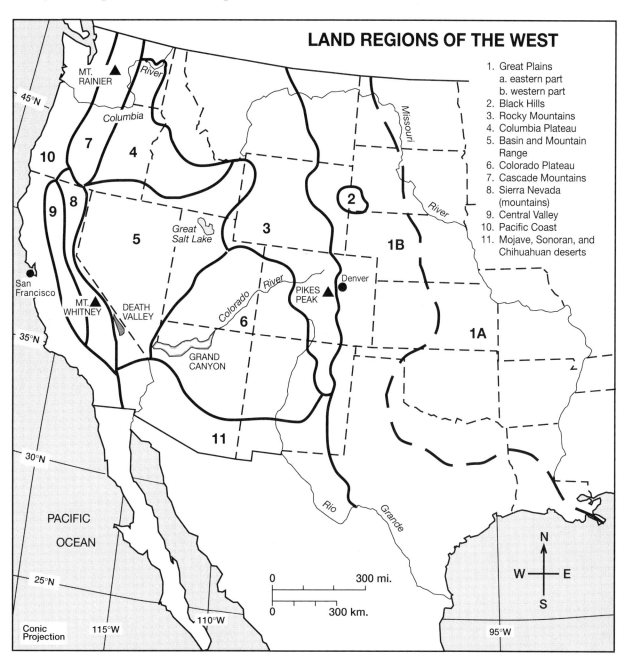

LAND REGIONS OF THE WEST

1. Great Plains
   a. eastern part
   b. western part
2. Black Hills
3. Rocky Mountains
4. Columbia Plateau
5. Basin and Mountain Range
6. Colorado Plateau
7. Cascade Mountains
8. Sierra Nevada (mountains)
9. Central Valley
10. Pacific Coast
11. Mojave, Sonoran, and Chihuahuan deserts

1. What type of landform would you find in Regions 3, 5, 7, and 8? _____

2. In which region would you expect to find the driest climate? _____

_____

3. How many land regions would you cross traveling due west from Denver to San

Francisco? What are they? _____

_____

_____

4. In which land region is each of the following physical features located?

   a. Pikes Peak _____

   b. Grand Canyon _____

   c. Death Valley _____

   d. Mt. Rainier _____

5. Which is the smallest land region shown on the map? _____

6. Approximately which line of longitude forms the dividing line between the eastern part

of the Great Plains and the western part? _____

7. *Sierra Nevada* means "snow-covered mountain range" in Spanish. What does this tell

you about the history of this region? _____

8. Geographic Theme: Regions What advantages did western land regions offer settlers
in the late 1800s? (See textbook pages 553–557.)

_____

_____

_____

_____

_____

_____

_____

_____

CHAPTER 24   **Map Practice**
Politics and Reform   **Geography Worksheet 47**

A. Use the map of United States cities and states on textbook pages
R12–R13 to locate the following states. Label these features on the
Outline Map on the back of this page.

States

Kansas	Ohio	Massachusetts	Oklahoma
Pennsylvania	Wisconsin	Texas	Indiana
Nebraska	Minnesota	California	Tennessee
Illinois	Wyoming	Utah	Florida

B. Use the maps on textbook pages 591 and 593 and the text in
Chapter 24 to answer the following questions.

1. Which state was the first to grant women full suffrage? _____

   In what year? _____

2. Which region of the country was most in favor of women's suffrage? _____

3. By 1919, which states had not yet granted women any suffrage rights? _____

   _____

   _____

4. What law guaranteed women's suffrage throughout the United States? _____

5. In which city did the Tweed Ring operate? _____

6. In what regions of the country was the Populist movement the strongest? _____

   _____

7. Robert M. La Follette was elected governor of which state in 1900? _____

8. Who were the candidates from each party for President in 1912? _____

   _____

   _____

9. How many electoral votes did Taft receive? _____

   How many states did he win? _____

CHAPTER 24: Outline Map

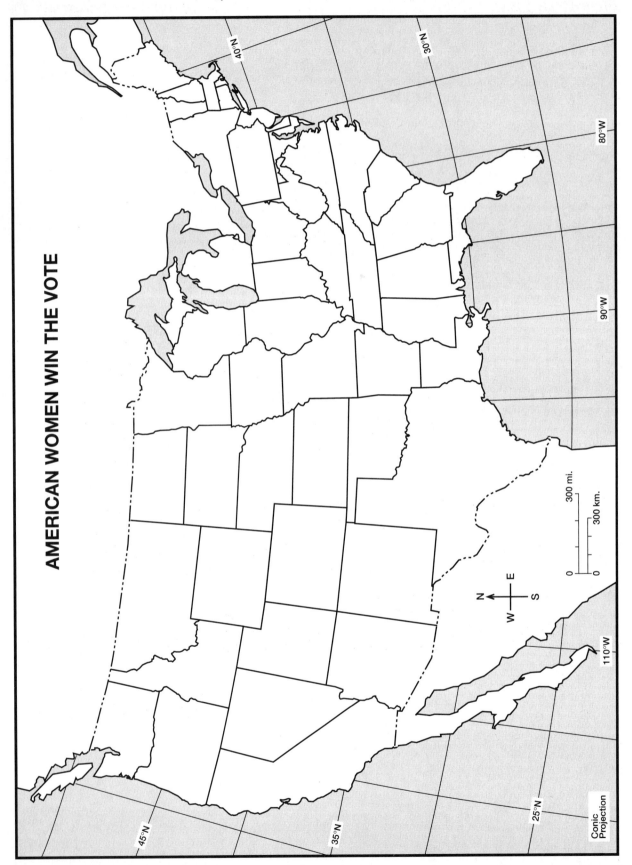

AMERICAN WOMEN WIN THE VOTE

Name _____   Date _____

American cities grew rapidly during the late 1800s. The maps below provide information about urban growth between 1860 and 1900. Study them and answer the questions that follow.

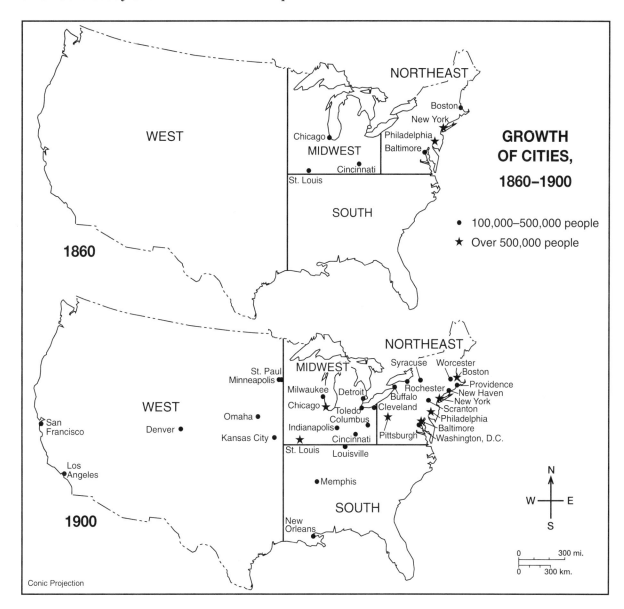

1. In which regions were most major cities located in 1860? _____

2. Which cities had populations greater than 500,000 in 1860? _____

3. How many cities had populations greater than 500,000 in 1900? _____

4. How many cities in the West had populations of 100,000 or more in 1900? _____

5. Which region had the slowest rate of urban growth between 1860 and 1900? _____

6. Which city in the Northeast grew from less than 100,000 people to more than 500,000

people between 1860 and 1900? _____

7. Geographic Theme: Movement What factors caused the rapid growth of American cities during the late 1800s? Why did cities grow more rapidly in some regions than in others?

_____

_____

_____

_____

_____

_____

_____

CHAPTER 25
Expansion in Latin America

A. Use the maps on textbook pages 609 and R16–R17 to locate the following countries, possessions, and bodies of water. Label them on the Outline Map on the back of this page.

Countries and possessions			*Bodies of Water*
United States	El Salvador	Cuba	Atlantic Ocean
Mexico	Nicaragua	Haiti	Pacific Ocean
Guatemala	Costa Rica	Dominican	Gulf of Mexico
British Honduras	Panama	Republic	Caribbean Sea
Honduras	Colombia	Puerto Rico	Panama Canal
	Venezuela		

B. Use the maps on textbook pages 609 and R16–R17 to answer the following questions.

1. Which Latin American country shares a border with the United States? _____

2. Which group of islands is located to the southeast of Florida? _____

_____

3. Which two countries share the same island in the Caribbean Sea? _____

_____

4. Which country is south of Honduras and north of Costa Rica? _____

5. Which island is closer to the mainland United States, Cuba or Puerto Rico?

_____

6. San José, located at 10°N latitude and 84°W longitude, is the capital of what Latin

American country? _____

7. A ship sailing directly south from Puerto Rico would reach the coast of what Latin

American country? _____

8. According to the map on textbook page 609, where was a U.S. naval base established in

1903? _____

9. Why were United States businesses interested in Latin America in the 1800s? (See text-

book, page 609.) _____

_____

_____

CHAPTER 25: Outline Map

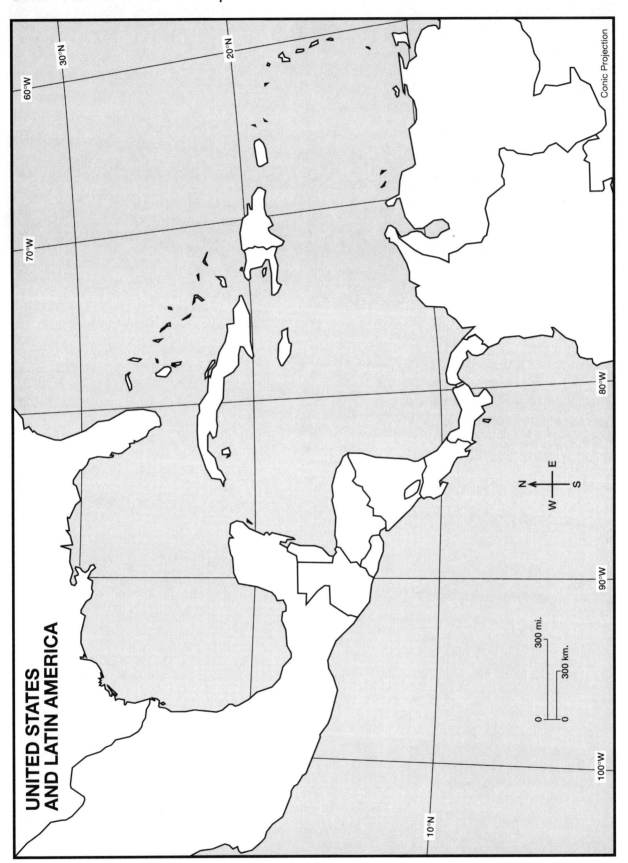

AMERICA'S PAST AND PROMISE
© Houghton Mifflin Company. All rights reserved.

Name _____ Date _____

The Panama Canal took ten years to complete. Although the route through Panama was shorter than the proposed route through Nicaragua, it was more difficult to build. A system of locks was needed to raise and lower ships through the canal's different levels. The map below shows the completed canal. Study the map and answer the questions that follow.

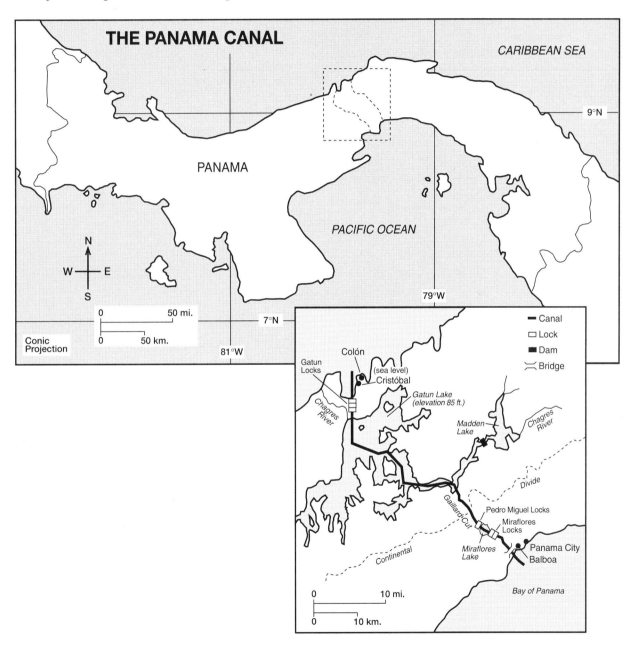

THE PANAMA CANAL

CARIBBEAN SEA

9°N

PANAMA

PACIFIC OCEAN

79°W

N
W — E
S

0   50 mi.
0   50 km.

Conic
Projection

81°W   7°N

Colón

Gatun
Locks

(sea level)
Cristóbal

Gatun Lake
(elevation 85 ft.)

Chagres
River

Madden
Lake

Chagres
River

Divide

Gaillard Cut

Pedro Miguel Locks
Miraflores
Locks

Miraflores
Lake

Panama City
Balboa

Continental

Bay of Panama

0   10 mi.
0   10 km.

▬ Canal
☐ Lock
▮ Dam
‿ Bridge

1. Use a ruler and the map's scale bar to find the approximate length of the Panama Canal.

_____

2. How many locks does the canal have? _____

3. Which cities are located at the Caribbean end of the canal? _____

At the Pacific end? _____

4. A ship passing through the canal from Cristóbal to Balboa travels in what direction?

_____

5. How many feet must a ship be raised to sail from the Caribbean Sea into Gatun Lake?

_____

6. Gatun Lake and Madden Lake were formed by damming which river? _____

7. What topographic obstacle made the Gaillard Cut necessary? _____

8. Geographic Theme: Place Describe the physical characteristics that made Panama a poor choice for a canal site. Then discuss the work that was necessary to make the Panama Canal one of the greatest engineering feats of all time. (Use the map above with textbook pages 608–609.)

_____

_____

_____

_____

_____

_____

_____

_____

_____

_____

CHAPTER 26   **Map Practice**
The United States in the 1920s   **Geography Worksheet 51**

A. Use the map of United States cities and states on textbook pages
R12–R13 to locate the following cities and states. Label these places
on the Outline Map on the back of this page.

Cities   *States*
Boston   Massachusetts   Tennessee
Washington, D.C.   Connecticut   Georgia
New York City   Ohio   Indiana
New Orleans   Wyoming   California
Detroit   Vermont   Michigan
Chicago   New York

B. Use the text of Chapter 26 to answer the following questions.

1. In what city was there a major police strike while Calvin Coolidge was governor?

_____

2. From where in the United States did President Harding come? _____

3. From what region of the United States did President Coolidge come? _____

4. What was the name given to the group of friends and advisers Harding brought with

him to Washington? Why were they given this name? _____

_____

5. In which state were the government-owned oil reserves that became the subject of cor-

ruption within the Harding administration? _____

6. Where did Lindbergh begin his historic flight? What was so impressive about

Lindbergh's flight? _____

_____

7. In what city was the Ford Motor Company located? _____

8. In what city did jazz first appear in the late 1800s? _____

9. In which state did the conflict over the teaching of the theory of evolution draw national

attention? _____

CHAPTER 26: Outline Map

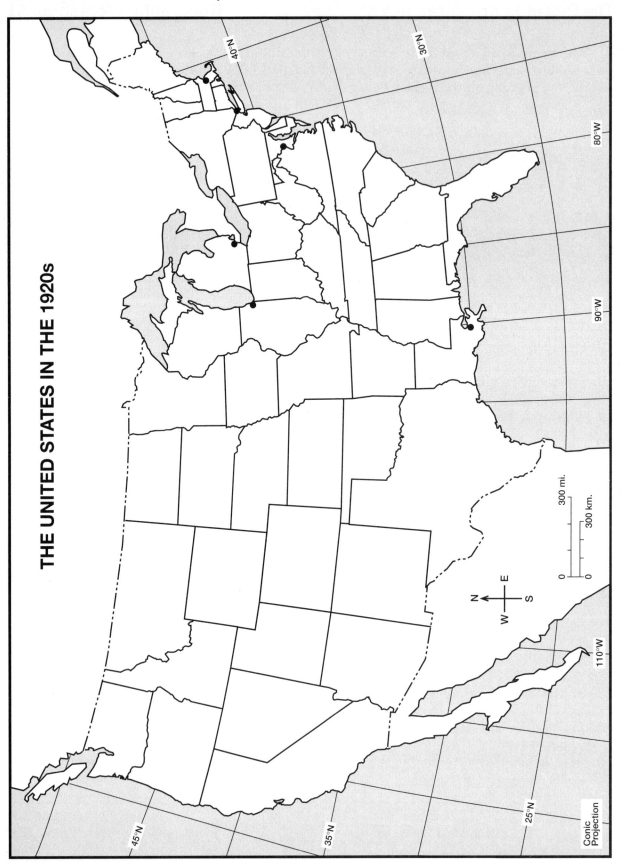

THE UNITED STATES IN THE 1920s

CHAPTER 26
The Palestine Mandate

During the early 1920s, as the United States returned to isola-
tion, the League of Nations dealt with such issues as the
breakup of the defeated Ottoman Empire. The League put different areas of the Middle East (called mandates) under foreign
control. Syria became a French mandate; Iraq and Palestine
became mandates of Great Britain. As the map below shows, the
Palestine Mandate was altered later. Study the map and answer
the questions that follow.

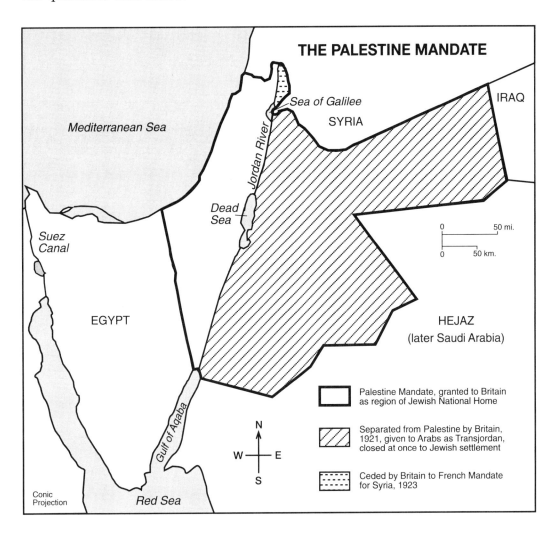

1. What type of line does this map use to indicate the original Palestine Mandate?

_____

2. How did the mandated area change in 1921? In 1923? _____

_____

_____

_____

3. Use a ruler and the map's scale bar to determine the approximate length of Palestine in

1923 from north to south. _____

4. About how many miles wide was Palestine in 1923 at its widest point? _____

5. Which natural features formed part of Palestine's 1923 borders? _____

_____

_____

6. Which area was larger, Palestine in 1921 or Transjordan? _____

7. What are some of Palestine's geographic advantages? _____

_____

8. Geographic Theme: Location Look at the world map on textbook pages R16–R17.
After World War I, Great Britain also controlled the Suez Canal, large areas of Africa,
India, Burma, and Malaysia. Why, do you think, was Palestine known as "the geographi-
cal center of the British Empire"? What was its strategic value?

_____

_____

_____

_____

_____

_____

_____

_____

Name _____   Date _____

CHAPTER 27   **Map Practice**
The Great Depression   **Geography Worksheet 53**

A. Use the maps on textbook pages 662, 665, and R12–R13 to locate
the following cities and states. Label these places on the Outline
Map on the back of this page.

Cities   *States*
New York City   Amarillo   Kansas   Nebraska
Chicago   San Francisco   California   Colorado
Philadelphia   Dodge City   Texas   South Dakota
Washington, D.C. Knoxville   Oklahoma   Wyoming
Los Angeles   New Mexico   Tennessee

B. Use the maps on textbook pages 662 and 665 to answer the following questions.

1. Which states had areas served by TVA electric power? _____

_____

_____

2. In which state was the Watts Bar dam located? _____

   In which state was the Guntersville dam located? _____

3. Which states experienced damage as a result of dust storms during the 1930s?

_____

_____

4. Which states had areas of severe damage? _____

_____

5. Where did many of the migrants from the Dust Bowl move in hope of finding a better

   life? _____

6. What were the two main migration routes traveled by migrants heading west?

_____

_____

7. What was the Bonus Army? To what city did they march and why? _____

_____

_____

CHAPTER 27: Outline Map

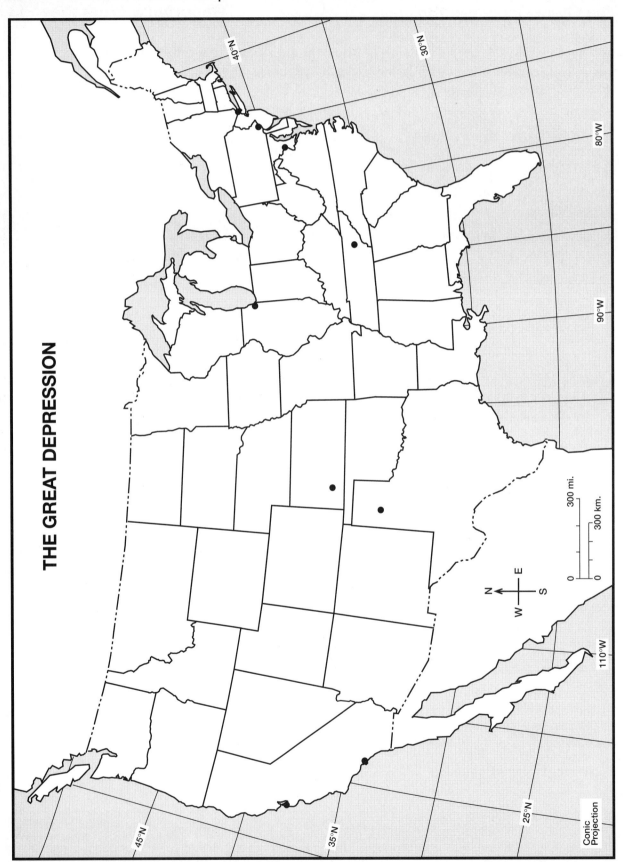

THE GREAT DEPRESSION

CHAPTER 27
The Growth of Farm Tenancy

During the Great Depression, many farmers, unable to pay their mortgages, lost their farms. They became tenants on the land they once owned, and paid rent to the banks that had repossessed their property. Study the map below which shows the growth of farm tenancy and answer the questions that follow.

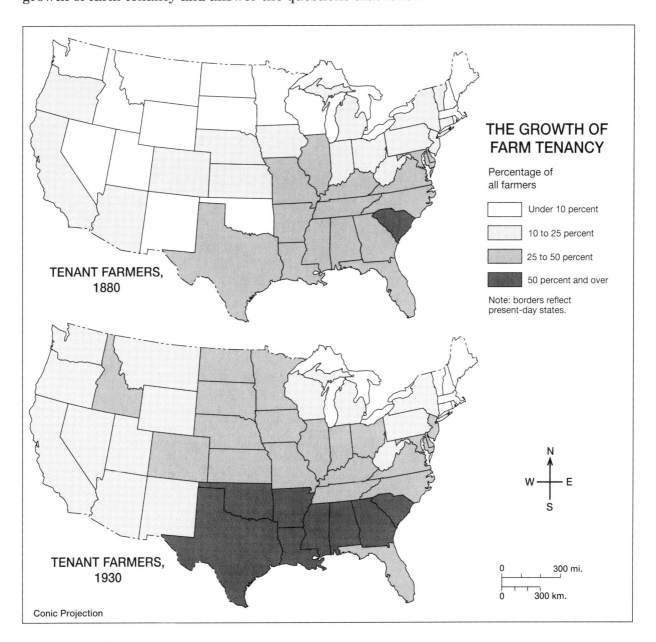

THE GROWTH OF
FARM TENANCY

Percentage of
all farmers

Under 10 percent

10 to 25 percent

25 to 50 percent

50 percent and over

Note: borders reflect
present-day states.

TENANT FARMERS,
1880

TENANT FARMERS,
1930

Conic Projection

1. In 1880, in which state were more than 50 percent of the farmers tenant farmers?

_____

2. In which region of the country was farm tenancy the highest in 1880? _____

In 1930? _____

3. In which region of the country did farm tenancy decline somewhat between 1880 and

1930? _____

4. Describe what happened to farm tenancy in the West between 1880 and 1930.

_____

_____

_____

5. Based on the information in these maps, do you think the number of American farmers who owned their own farms between 1880 and 1930 rose, declined, or stayed the same? Why?

_____

_____

_____

_____

6. Geographic Theme: Interactions The South suffered from a severe drought in 1930. Much of the Great Plains received little rainfall between 1933 and 1936. What changes would you expect to see in a map showing farm tenancy in 1936? Why?

_____

_____

_____

_____

_____

_____

_____

_____

CHAPTER 28
Americans, 1900–1940

Map Practice
Geography Worksheet 55

A. Use the Atlas maps on textbook pages R12–R13 and R14–R15 to locate the following states, cities, and bodies of water. Label these features on the Outline Map on the back of this page.

States	*Cities*	*Bodies of Water*
New York	Detroit	Gulf of Mexico
California	Chicago	Atlantic Ocean
Texas	Harlem	Pacific Ocean
Washington	Philadelphia	Lake Erie
Oregon	St. Louis	Lake Ontario
		Lake Huron
		Lake Michigan
		Lake Superior

B. Use the Outline Map and the text of Chapter 28 to answer the following questions.

1. What factors forced the United States to struggle with the identity of the nation? (See page 677.) _____

_____

2. From where did most immigrants to the United States come before the 1860s?

_____

3. How did the pattern of immigration change after 1860? _____

_____

4. In what areas did most Italian immigrants settle between 1880 and 1920? _____

_____

5. Where did most Jewish immigrants settle? _____

6. What is anti-Semitism? What did Jewish immigrants do to overcome it? _____

_____

_____

7. Explain why assimilation was often more difficult for Asian immigrants than for

European immigrants. _____

_____

CHAPTER 28: Outline Map

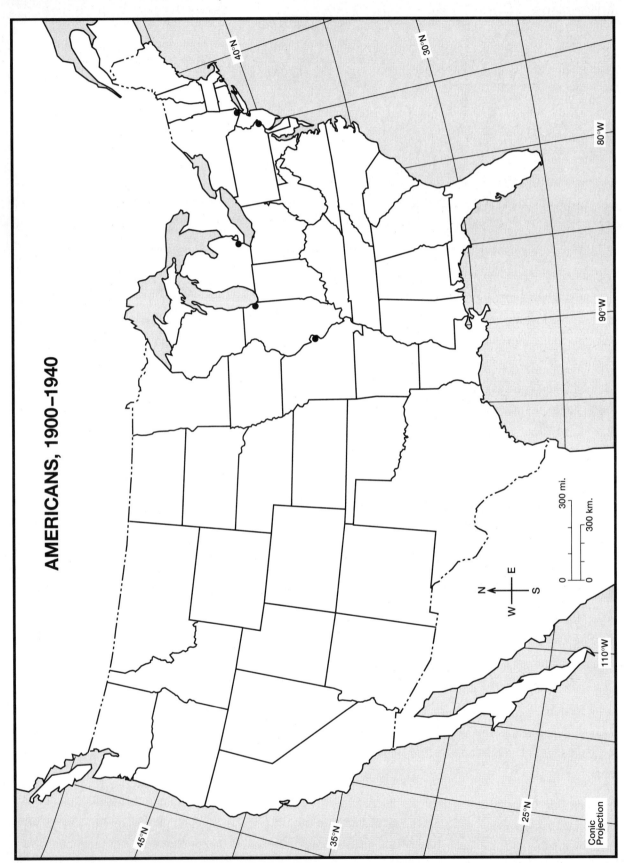

AMERICANS, 1900–1940

Name _____   Date _____

CHAPTER 28   **Geography Challenge**
Immigration Restrictions in the 1920s   **Geography Worksheet 56**

Immigration to the United States slowed dramatically after
World War I. The change resulted from laws enacted in the
1920s limiting immigration. The bar graph below shows where
most immigrants came from before and after the immigration
laws changed. Study the graph and answer the questions that
follow.

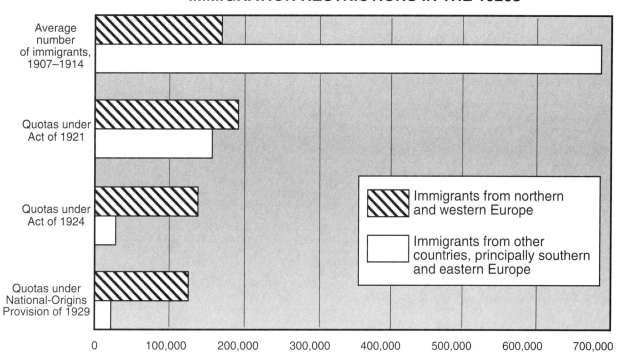

IMMIGRATION RESTRICTIONS IN THE 1920s

1. About how many immigrants from countries outside of northern and western Europe

   came to the United States in an average year between 1907 and 1914? _____

2. What was the greatest number of immigrants from southern and eastern Europe that

   could come to the United States in 1922? _____

3. How did the immigration laws of the 1920s affect immigration from southern and eastern Europe? Compare immigration from this region in 1929 to immigration fifteen years
   earlier.

   _____

   _____

   _____

4. How did the number of immigrants from northern and western Europe change as a

   result of the Act of 1921? _____

5. When, according to the graph, did the sharpest drop occur in the number of immigrants

   from northern and western Europe? _____

6. What was the total number of immigrants to the United States in an average year

   between 1907 and 1914? _____

7. How many immigrants could come to the United States in 1925? _____

8. How did the immigration laws of the 1920s affect total immigration? _____

   _____

9. **Geographic Theme: Movement** What conclusions can you draw from these graphs
   regarding American attitudes towards immigration during the 1920s? What are some
   possible reasons why Americans felt this way? Under what kinds of circumstances do
   people become resistant to admitting newcomers to their land?

   _____

   _____

   _____

   _____

   _____

   _____

   _____

   _____

CHAPTER 29   **Map Practice**
The Allies Win in Europe   **Geography Worksheet 57**

A. Use the map on textbook page 707 to locate the following bodies
of water and countries. Label these places on the Outline Map on the
back of this page.

Bodies of Water		*Countries*		
Atlantic Ocean	Rhône River	Great Britain	Spain	Sweden
North Sea	Elbe River	France	Switzerland	Finland
Mediterranean	Danube River	Germany	Poland	Turkey
Sea	Volga River	Italy	Czechoslovakia	Egypt
Black Sea	Don River	Soviet Union	Tunisia	Algeria
Baltic Sea		Portugal	Norway	

B. Use the map on textbook page 707 to answer the following questions.

1. Which major Allied nations appear on the map? _____

   _____

2. Which European nations remained neutral during World War II? _____

   _____

   _____

3. According to the map, how was France divided during the war? _____

   _____

   _____

4. Which European nations were Axis nations? _____

5. Describe the movement of Allied troops, starting in 1944, that eventually defeated the

   Axis in Europe. _____

   _____

Use the map on textbook page 708 to answer questions 6–7.

6. Which body of water divides Great Britain from France? _____

7. The Germans were given false information to make them think that the D-Day assault
   would come at Calais. For what geographic reason might they have believed this?

   _____

   _____

CHAPTER 29: Outline Map

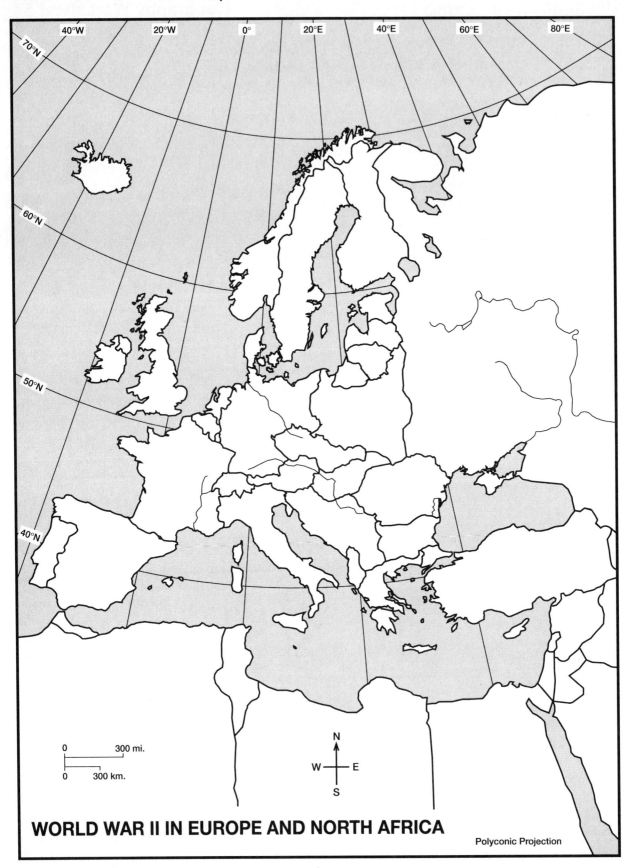

0   300 mi.

0   300 km.

N
W   E
S

WORLD WAR II IN EUROPE AND NORTH AFRICA

Polyconic Projection

Name _____ Date _____

In 1942 the Soviet Union, worn out by its heroic resistance against the German army, pleaded with the other Allies to form a second front against the Axis. The United States and Britain were reluctant to assault the European mainland. Instead, they attacked Axis-held territory in North Africa. There they met one of the most able German generals of the war, Erwin Rommel, "the Desert Fox." Study the map below and answer the questions that follow.

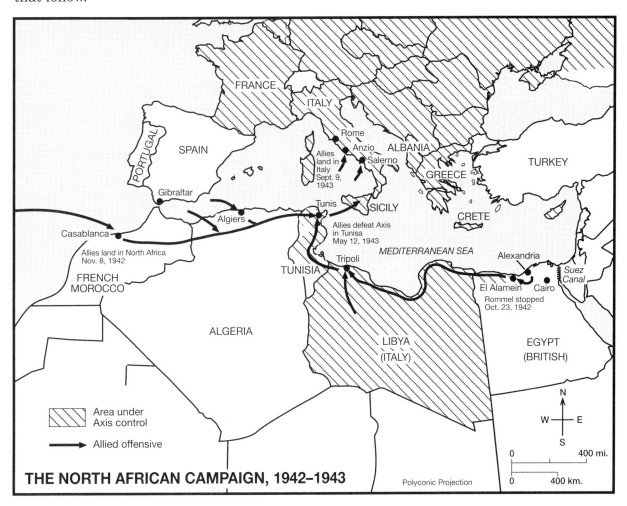

THE NORTH AFRICAN CAMPAIGN, 1942–1943

1. Which African and European nations labeled on the map were under Axis control in

1942? _____

_____

_____

2. What important waterway did Rommel seek to control in his North Africa Campaign?

_____

3. Use a ruler and the map's scale bar to find how far from Cairo Rommel's Afrika Korps were when they were stopped. What was the location and date of this turning point in the war?

_____

_____

4. What does the map show the Allies did in November of 1942? _____

_____

5. How long alter Rommel's defeat did it take for the Allies to attain victory in North

Africa? Where did this happen? When? _____

_____

6. Geographic Theme: Movement After the North African victory, Winston Churchill said that "the soft underbelly of Europe" lay open to Allied attack. What did he mean? What did the Allies do next to illustrate his words?

_____

_____

_____

_____

_____

_____

_____

_____

CHAPTER 30
The Vietnam War

**Map Practice
Geography Worksheet 59**

A. Use the map on textbook page 730 to locate the following bodies of water, nations, and cities. Label these places on the Outline Map on the back of this page.

Bodies of Water	*Nations*	*Cities*
Gulf of Tonkin	China	Dien Bien Phu
South China Sea	Laos	Hanoi
Mekong River	Thailand	Haiphong
Red River	Cambodia	Hué
	(Kampuchea)	Saigon
	North Vietnam	
	South Vietnam	

B. Use the map on textbook page 730 to answer the following questions.

1. Which natural feature forms much of the border between Laos and Thailand?

    _____

2. Which nations border Vietnam to the west? _____

3. Into which body of water does the Mekong River empty? _____

4. Into which body of water does the Red River empty? _____

5. Which cities would likely be affected by the flooding of the Red River?

    _____

6. Which major city is in the Mekong Delta area? _____

7. Use a ruler and the scale bar to determine the distance between Hanoi and Haiphong.

    _____

8. Where were the chief areas that the Saigon government controlled during the war?

    _____

    _____

9. Where were the chief areas of Vietcong control during the war? _____

    _____

CHAPTER 30: Outline Map

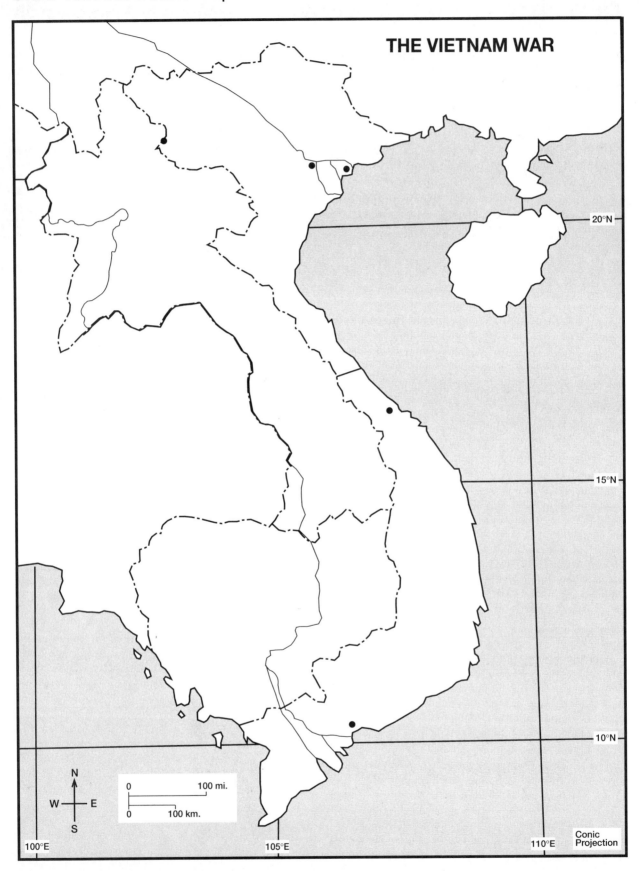

THE VIETNAM WAR

20°N

15°N

10°N

N
W — E
S

| 0 | 100 mi. |
| 0 | 100 km. |

100°E   105°E   110°E   Conic
Projection

Name _____ Date _____

The political map of the world changed rapidly in the years following World War II. Communist governments came to power in Eastern Europe and parts of Asia including China, the world's most populous country. Study the map and table below and answer the questions that follow.

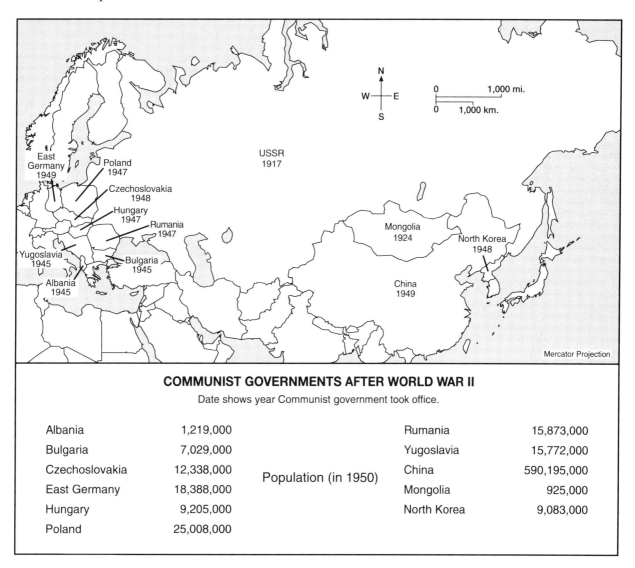

COMMUNIST GOVERNMENTS AFTER WORLD WAR II

Date shows year Communist government took office.

	Population (in 1950)		
Albania	1,219,000	Rumania	15,873,000
Bulgaria	7,029,000	Yugoslavia	15,772,000
Czechoslovakia	12,338,000	China	590,195,000
East Germany	18,388,000	Mongolia	925,000
Hungary	9,205,000	North Korea	9,083,000
Poland	25,008,000		

1. How many nations in Eastern Europe had Communist governments by 1946? Name them.

_____

_____

2. In which nations did Communist governments gain power in 1949?

_____

_____

3. Which were the two most populous Communist nations in Eastern Europe by 1950?

Which was the least populous? _____

_____

4. Which was greater, the total population of Communist nations in Eastern Europe or the

total population of Communist nations in Asia? _____

5. When he took control of nations in Eastern Europe, Soviet leader Stalin claimed that the Soviet Union needed friendly states on its borders as protection from the West. Which Eastern European nations shared a land border with the Soviet Union?

_____

6. Geographic Theme: Regions How does the information on the map and table justify President Truman's policy of containment? Explain. (See textbook, page 732.)

_____

_____

_____

_____

_____

_____

_____

A. Use the map of United States cities and states on textbook pages R12–R13 to locate the following bodies of water and states. Label these features on the Outline Map on the back of this page.

Bodies of Water	*States*		
Atlantic Ocean	South Carolina	Louisiana	Arizona
Pacific Ocean	Georgia	Texas	Nevada
Gulf of Mexico	Florida	New Mexico	California
	Alabama	Colorado	Alaska
	Mississippi	Utah	Hawaii

B. Use the map on textbook page 744 and the Outline Map to answer the following questions.

1. Which states show a population increase of more than 100 percent? _____

_____

2. Which states east of the Mississippi River show a 35–50 percent gain? _____

_____

3. Which states with a 51–100 percent gain are not in the West? _____

_____

4. Which of the states that border the Atlantic Ocean or the Gulf of Mexico do not show a

gain of 35 percent or more? _____

_____

_____

5. With the exception of two states, all of the Great Lakes states experienced about the same degree of growth. Into which category do they fall? Which states were the exceptions? How were these states different?

_____

_____

6. Which northeastern states had the smallest population gains (0–34 percent)? _____

_____

_____

CHAPTER 31: Outline Map

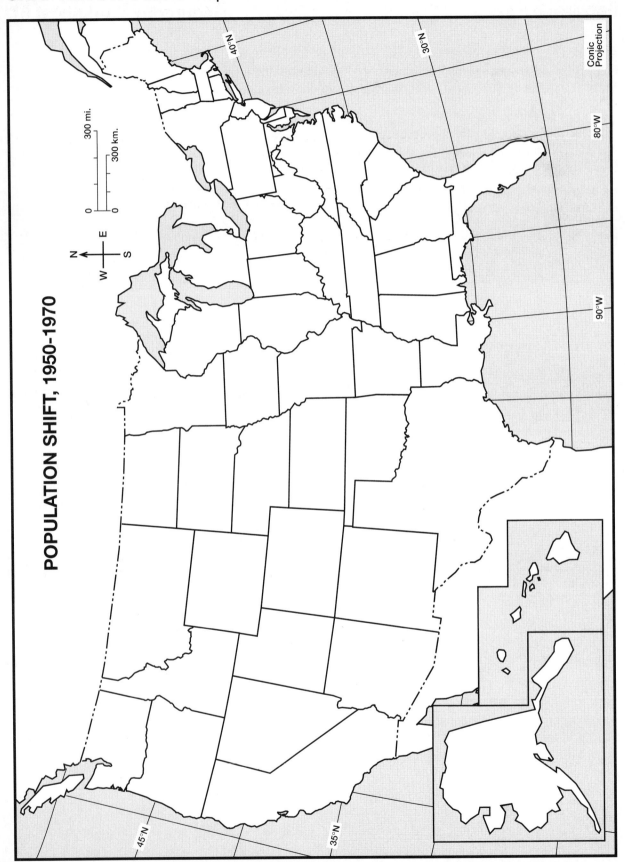

POPULATION SHIFT, 1950-1970

300 mi.

300 km.

N
W E
S

Conic Projection

40°N

30°N

80°W

90°W

45°N

35°N

CHAPTER 31
Shifting Centers of Population

Geography Challenge
Geography Worksheet 62

Every ten years beginning in 1790, the United States has taken
a census—a count of all the people in the country. Using information from the census, experts known as *demographers* can
locate the "population center" of the country. The population center has exactly the same number of Americans living north,
south, east, and west of it. This map shows how the population
center of the United States shifted between 1790 and 1980.
Study the map and answer the questions that follow.

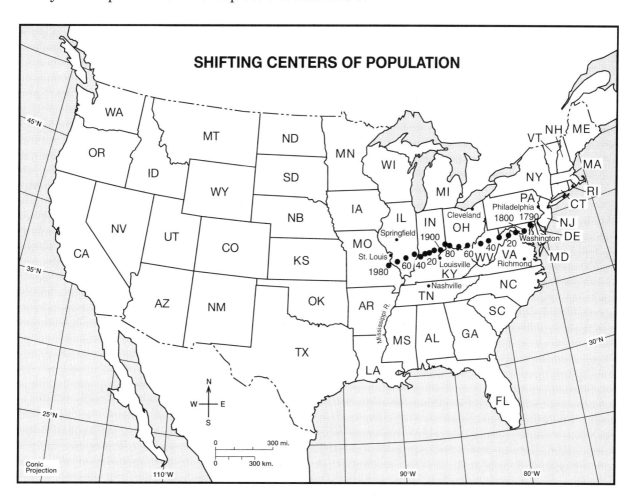

1. What is the earliest date shown on the map? _____

2. Circle the statement that is correct for 1790.   **(A)** More than half the people in the
   country lived west of the Mississippi River.   **(B)** More than half the people in the country lived south of Virginia.   **(C)** About half the people in the country lived east of
   Maryland.

3. In what present-day state was the population center located in 1840? _____

4. To what city was the population center closest in 1800? _____

5. In what state did the population center remain longest? _____

6. Which year's census showed that the population center had crossed the Mississippi

River? _____

7. In what directions does the map show the population center to be moving? _____

8. Use a ruler and the map's scale bar to determine approximately how far the population

center moved between 1790 and 1980. _____

9. Geographic Theme: Movement Explain how each of the following events probably
affected the movement of the population center: (a) the discovery of gold in California in
1848; (b) completion of the transcontinental railroad in 1869; (c) a series of droughts on
the western plains in the late 1880s and 1890s.

_____

_____

_____

_____

_____

_____

_____

_____

_____

_____

CHAPTER 32
The Civil Rights Movement

Map Practice
Geography Worksheet 63

A. Use the map of the United States cities and states on pages R12–R13 to locate the following states and cities. Label these features on the Outline Map on the back of this page.

States		*Cities*	
Kansas	Louisiana	Topeka	Washington, D.C.
Alabama	Virginia	Montgomery	Los Angeles
Arkansas	Florida	Birmingham	New York
North Carolina	California	Little Rock	Chicago
Tennessee	New York	Memphis	Detroit
Georgia	Illinois	Nashville	San Francisco
Mississippi		Atlanta	

B. Use the Outline Map and the text of Chapter 32 to answer the following questions.

1. Many historians consider a famous bus boycott to be the beginning of the activist phase of the civil rights movement. Where did this boycott take place? _____

2. In which city and state did the challenge to segregation lead to a landmark Supreme Court ruling calling for integration of public schools? _____

   What was the name of this court case? _____

3. To which city and state did President Eisenhower order troops in 1957 to enforce the integration of a high school? _____

4. Where did the first lunch counter sit-in take place? _____

5. Which African American civil rights group organized a series of freedom rides through segregated southern cities? _____

6. What were the main points of the Civil Rights Act of 1964? (See textbook, page 769.)

   _____

   _____

7. How did César Chavez help migrant workers in the 1960s? (See textbook, pages 772–773.) _____

   _____

   _____

CHAPTER 32: Outline Map

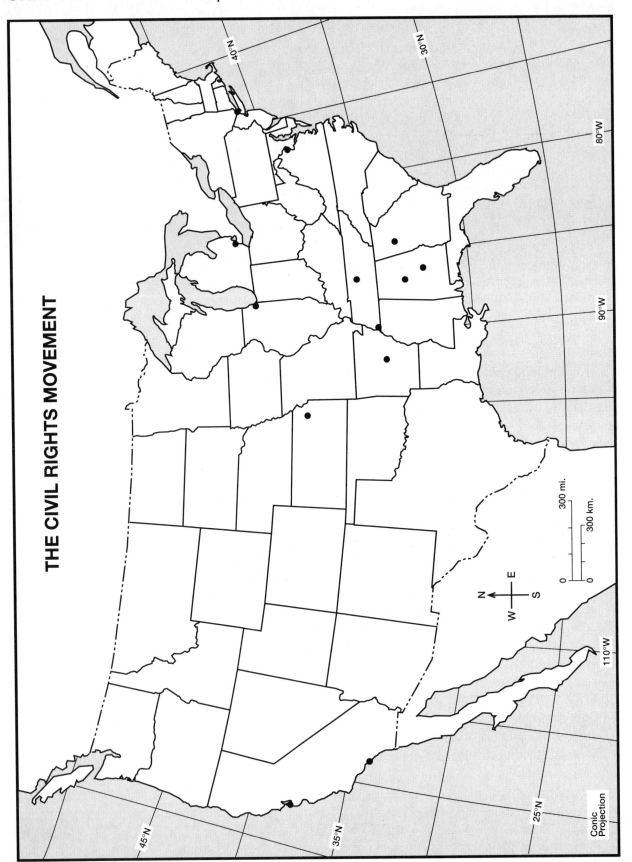

THE CIVIL RIGHTS MOVEMENT

CHAPTER 32   **Geography Challenge**
School Integration, 1954–1960   **Geography Worksheet 64**

In 1954, after years of legal action, the Supreme Court ruled
that the "separate but equal" doctrine that underlay racial segregation in the schools was unconstitutional. The Court called
for integration "with all deliberate speed." Study the map and
answer the questions that follow.

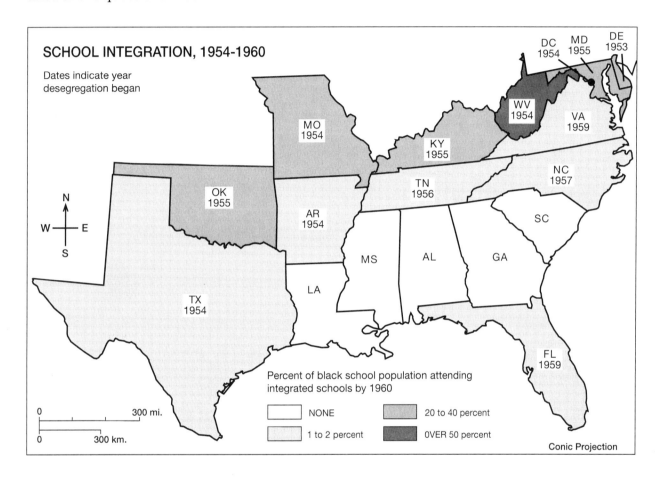

1. Which state on the map had begun to integrate its public schools before the Supreme

Court ruling in 1954? In what year did this happen? _____

_____

2. Of the states that integrated their schools before 1960, which were the first to integrate

following the court decision? Which were the last? _____

_____

_____

3. Which other location, not a state, also began integration in 1954? _____

_____

4. Which states still had not begun to integrate their school systems by 1960? _____

_____

_____

5. Which states had integrated from 20 to 40 percent of their schoolchildren by 1960?

_____

_____

6. What percentage of integration had been achieved by West Virginia by 1960? _____

7. Geographic Theme: Regions Which states resisted school integration most strongly?
Where are these states located? How do you think the economic and social history of this
region influenced its resistance to segregation?

_____

_____

_____

_____

_____

_____

_____

_____

CHAPTER 33
The Middle East

A. Use the map on textbook page 790 to locate the following countries and bodies of water. Label them on the Outline Map on the back
of this page.

Countries

			Water Areas
Saudi Arabia	Libya	Oman	Red Sea
Iraq	Egypt	Bahrain	Nile River
Israel	Turkey	United Arab	Persian Gulf
Syria	Sudan	Emirates	Mediterranean
Lebanon	Kuwait	Qatar	Sea
Iran	Cyprus		Arabian Sea
Jordan	Yemen		Gulf of Oman

B. Use textbook pages 788–791 to answer the following questions.

1. Which nation borders Israel to the North? _____

   Which nations border Israel to the east? _____

2. Name the nations that border the Persian Gulf. _____

   _____

   _____

3. In which nation is the Suez Canal located? Which bodies of water does it connect?

   _____

4. Which Middle Eastern nation invaded Kuwait in 1990? _____

5. What actions did the United Nations take after the invasion of Kuwait?

   _____

   _____

   _____

6. In which European nation did ethnic hatreds cause four republics to declare indepen-

   dence and wars to break out? _____

7. In which African nation did civil war and famine erupt in the early 1990s?

   _____

8. Which African nation made progress toward democracy by enacting major reforms and

   working for an end to racial hatred? _____

CHAPTER 33: Outline Map

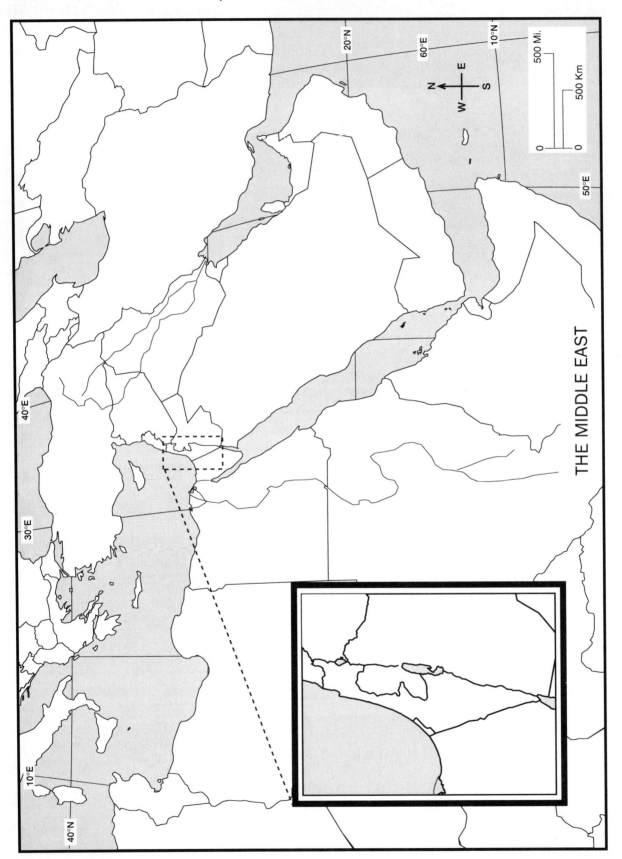

THE MIDDLE EAST

20°N

60°E

10°N

500 Mi.

N
W ← E
S

500 Km

50°E

40°E

30°E

10°E

40°N

Name _____ Date _____

With the end of the Cold War, new conflicts and new opportunities for peace arose around the world. Study the map of the world below. Use the map with Chapter 33 to answer the questions that follow.

THE WORLD AFTER THE COLD WAR

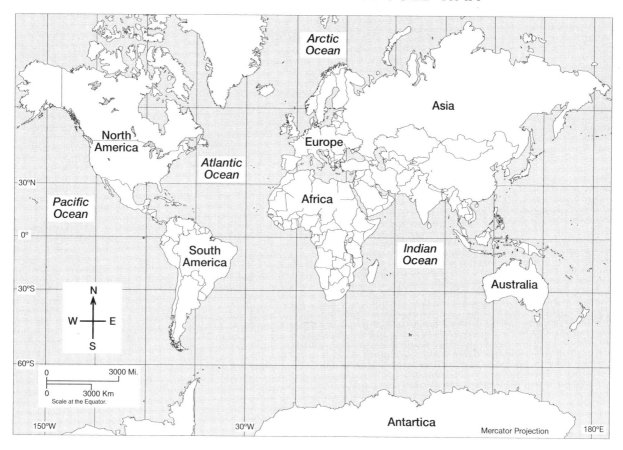

1. Which nation borders the United States to the north? To the south? _____

2. What historic trade agreement was made between the United States., Canada, and

   Mexico in 1993? _____

3. How was this trade agreement a sign of changes in the world economy? _____

   _____

   _____

4. What role did the United States play in Operation Desert Storm? _____

   _____

5. What did the PLO want for Palestinians living under Israeli rule? _____

6. What steps did Israel and the PLO make toward peace in 1993? _____

_____

_____

7. Which two men were awarded the Nobel Peace Prize in 1993? What were their

accomplishments? _____

_____

_____

8. Geographic Theme: Interactions What environmental challenges does the world
face today? What steps have been taken to confront these challenges?

_____

_____

_____

_____

_____

_____

_____

_____

_____

_____

Answers

CHAPTER 1

Worksheet 1

1. Asia
2. By walking to North America over Beringia during the last ice age, or by boat
3. Rocky Mountains, Andes
4. Asia and North America
5. The warming of the earth caused the ocean to rise and cover Beringia.
6. Bering Strait
7. The domestication of plants gave people a stable food supply, which enabled them to build permanent settlements and develop more complex societies, governments, and cultures.

Worksheet 2

1. Inupiat, Inuit, Cree, Aleut
2. Eastern Woodlands
3. Great Plains, Eastern Woodlands, Southeast
4. Southeast, Mexico and Mesoamerica
5. Caribbean, Amazon, Andes
6. Mexico and Mesoamerica
7. Andes
8. Great Basin
9. The Northwest Coast Indians lived off the sea. They harvested salmon from coastal streams every summer and fall. They also ate shellfish, seals, otters, and whales. The huge trees of the Northwest Coast area enabled the people to make great use of wood for houses, boats and hats, and bark for capes and mats. Wood was also used to make wooden boxes for cooking and to make intricate carvings and totem poles.

CHAPTER 2

Worksheet 3

1. The Sahara is the world's largest desert. It is located in northern Africa.
2. Savannas
3. The drying of the Sahara caused people living there to move to lands that could sustain them. This led to the development of distinct peoples and cultures.
4. The Nile River
5. Nubia
6. Hunting, fishing, herding cattle, and later, farming. Nubians also made livings through trade and ironworking.
7. Caravans carried goods from Kush to ports on the Red Sea and Mediterranean Sea. From there, the goods traveled to Arabia, India, and even China.
8. By growing crops suited to their climate, such as wheat, and through the spread of iron-making.

Worksheet 4

1. Mali, Songhai
2. Songhai
3. Ghana
4. Songhai
5. Mali; Timbuktu was famous for its mosques, royal palace, and its schools.
6. West Africa's warm tropical climate caused people to loose salt in perspiration. They needed to add salt to their diets to stay healthy.
7. Islam spread westward from Arabia across North Africa to the shores of the Atlantic Ocean. It was brought by traders southward across the Sahara after the year 1000.
8. With the spread of Islam, the African slave trade increased. Slaves were taken to Arabia, Persia, and other Muslim lands.
9. The riches of the Islamic world convinced many to become Muslim to increase their status in society. As contact with Muslim traders increased, many Africans learned to read and write Arabic, the language of Islam, which helped Islamic beliefs take hold. Also, many aspects of Islam were compatible with traditional African practices.

CHAPTER 3

Worksheet 5

1. Europe, Spain, Palos
2. West, East
3. San Salvador and Hispaniola
4. The voyage of 1498 took him to the northern coast of South America.
5. Puerto Rico
6. The voyage of 1502
7. He learned deep sea navigation and noticed that winter winds off North Africa blew from the east.

Worksheet 6

1. Norway, Sweden, Denmark
2. South, east, west
3. They traveled mainly by sea rather than overland.
4. North Sea, Atlantic Ocean, Mediterranean Sea, Black Sea
5. England, Ireland, Spain, France, Germany, Italy
6. Iceland
7. Approximately 70° N latitude

8. Greenland

9. Viking raids often devastated the land and the people. Threatened by invasions, Europeans turned to feudalism for survival. Feudalism was an economic, political, and social system that provided a way for people to live off the land.

CHAPTER 4

Worksheet 7

1. Ponce de León
2. De Soto
3. Cabrillo, Coronado
4. West from the Gulf of Mexico through present-day Texas, across the Rio Grande; south through Mexico to Culiacán.
5. Cabrillo
6. Ponce de León, Cabrillo
7. Caribbean Sea, Gulf of Mexico; Cabeza de Vaca
8. Cabeza de Vaca, Coronado

Worksheet 8

1. South to north
2. About 2,000 miles (3,200 kilometers)
3. The Caribbean islands, Central America, southern and eastern Mexico; the American Southwest and the coast of California
4. The Catholic Church; Spanish missionaries established the first European settlements in California and much of the American Southwest.
5. It decreased as millions of Indians died.
6. By 1550
7. It fell by over ten million.
8. 1550–1570
9. The Spanish wanted more land and valuable mineral resources. To extract those resources, they needed labor and tried to enslave the Indians for this purpose. The Indians died in massive numbers from diseases carried by the Spanish and were slaughtered by efficient European weapons.

CHAPTER 5

Worksheet 9

1. Hudson
2. Verrazano
3. Cartier, Champlain
4. Lake Huron, Lake Ontario
5. Southwestward across the Atlantic to the coast of North America; northward along the river that now bears his name, inland into present-day New York state

6. **a.** Holland, England **b.** France **c.** France **d.** France
7. A Northwest Passage to Asia
8. **a.** Hudson **b.** Champlain

Worksheet 10

1. Sir Walter Raleigh
2. 36°N; North
3. Pamlico Sound
4. Islands and sandbars
5. Saltwater marsh
6. About 55 miles (88 kilometers)
7. It had no harbor.
8. Roanoke Island had a mild climate. Settlers did not have to face bitter cold winters. The island was located near friendly Indians who helped settlers at first. Roanoke, however, lacked a safe harbor for ships. The English learned that better planning was needed to make a colony succeed. In addition to choosing a good location, settlers needed funds and supplies to face dangers such as enemy attacks, storms, and food shortages.

CHAPTER 6

Worksheet 11

1. New Hampshire
2. Jamestown: 1607, Philadelphia: 1682
3. About 190 miles (304 kilometers)
4. The Appalachian Mountains
5. English ships appeared off the coast of New Netherland in 1664. The Dutch colony surrendered without a fight.
6. Quakers. They believed that all people should live in peace and harmony and welcomed different religious and ethnic groups.
7. France, the Great Lakes were in French Territory; Spain, Florida and the Gulf coast were in Spanish Territory.

Worksheet 12

1. English and Scots-Irish
2. Scots-Irish
3. Jews
4. Along the Hudson River in New York state
5. Pennsylvania, Maryland, Georgia
6. North Carolina
7. Virginia and South Carolina
8. Groups of European immigrants brought different religious beliefs, values, languages, customs, and skills to the English colonies. Since immigrants tended to settle near people with the same national background, regions developed. Many Africans were brought to areas where large landowners used slave labor.

CHAPTER 7

Worksheet 13

1. Britain, Africa, West Indies
2. Rum and iron
3. West Indies
4. Sugar and molasses
5. Atlantic Ocean
6. Between the colonies and the West Indies
7. Northeast
8. North
9. Boston, New York, Philadelphia, Norfolk, Charles Town

Worksheet 14

1. The Southern Colonies
2. The New England Colonies
3. The Southern Colonies
4. The Appalachian Mountains
5. The Coastal Plain and the Appalachian Mountains
6. Shipbuilding and fishing industries
7. The Southern Colonies
8. The New England Colonies had rocky hills, the least fertile land in the colonies, and a short growing season, preventing them from depending solely on agriculture. Yet the colonies had excellent harbors and fishing grounds, and a large source of lumber for boats. The Southern Colonies, on the other hand, had the most fertile land and the longest growing season in the colonies, which made these colonies ideal for growing valuable warm-weather crops that could not be grown in Europe.

CHAPTER 8

Worksheet 15

1. Appalachian Mountains and Rocky Mountains
2. Gulf of Mexico
3. Missouri River
4. Southwest
5. West of the Mississippi River
6. About 2,300 miles (3,680 kilometers)
7. Arkansas River
8. Wisconsin River and Illinois River
9. 30°N, 90°W
10. It lies near the mouth of the Mississippi River.

Worksheet 16

1. Both
2. Before
3. After
4. Before
5. After
6. Before
7. Before
8. After
9. As a result of the 1763 Treaty of Paris, England gained all land between the Appalachian Mountains and the Mississippi River, except for New Orleans. England also controlled the St. Lawrence River, the Great Lakes, and the Ohio River. Therefore, England owned all land in the eastern half of North America from Hudson Bay to the Gulf of Mexico. The resources and waterways of that region provided England with opportunities for further settlement.

CHAPTER 9

Worksheet 17

1. Massachusetts
2. Georgia
3. Atlantic Ocean
4. Mississippi River
5. Proclamation Line of 1763
6. Land between the Appalachian Mountains and the Mississippi River and surrounding the Great Lakes
7. Great Lakes, Ohio River, Mississippi River
8. Around the Great Lakes
9. The Proclamation of 1763 prevented colonists from settling new lands west of the Appalachians. Land ownership was very important to colonists as a source of wealth and political power.

Worksheet 18

1. North Carolina, South Carolina, Georgia
2. Delaware, Maryland, Virginia, North Carolina
3. Cattle and grain, fish, whale products, ships, timber, furs
4. Rice, fish, meat
5. Furs, tobacco, naval stores, indigo, timber, rice, fish, meat
6. Iron and most other raw materials
7. All manufactured goods
8. British laws restricted the export of certain goods and prohibited the export of manufactured goods from the colonies. Britain permitted the colonies to import manufactured goods only from England. Foreign goods had to pass through English ports before going to the colonies. Britain controlled the colonial economy by limiting the movement of goods to and from the colonies.

CHAPTER 10

Worksheet 19

1. Spain
2. Britain, Spain, and Russia
3. The United States and Britain
4. a) The Great Lakes; b) The Mississippi River; c) the Ohio River; d) the Mississippi River
5. Spain
6. North of the Ohio River
7. Wisconsin, Indiana, Ohio, Illinois, Michigan, and part of Minnesota

Worksheet 20

1. Chesapeake Bay
2. York River
3. Cornwallis believed he could receive supplies by ship from New York.
4. French ships
5. American lines of defense and troops
6. French troops
7. Retreat across the York River was the only means of escape. With that route cut off, Cornwallis's position was hopeless.
8. Yorktown is located on a peninsula. A French fleet blocked escape to the east. American and French troops blocked escape to the south and west. Cornwallis was trapped, and bad weather prevented his only means of retreat across the York River.

CHAPTER 11

Worksheet 21

1. 30°N to 47°N; 67°W to 85°W
2. About 1,500 miles (2,400 Kilometers)
3. Vermont
4. St. Lawrence River, Lake Ontario, Lake Erie
5. The Ohio River
6. Political; They are straight lines and not shaped like natural (physical) features.
7. Physical (in this case the Savannah River)
8. Massachusetts
9. Philadelphia

Worksheet 22

1. Delaware, New Jersey, Georgia
2. Federalist position
3. Inland, in the more rural or recently developed region
4. Downstate
5. The Antifederalist territory, although larger in area, was far less populated than the Federalist territory.

6. There were no returns from these areas.
7. The population along the seaboard included business and trade interests, which depended upon a strong national government to support and protect their activities. The inland population consisted largely of farmers and small businessmen who feared taxation and governmental interference.

CHAPTER 12

Worksheet 23

1. New York City, Philadelphia, Washington, D.C.
2. Cincinnati, Pittsburgh
3. New Orleans
4. Spain; New Orleans was a port city at the mouth of the Mississippi River which allowed it to control trade passing down the river into the Gulf of Mexico. Westerners depended on this route to get their goods to market.
5. Virginia and Kentucky
6. Pennsylvania
7. Mississippi River
8. Washington, D.C.

Worksheet 24

1. Maryland, Virginia
2. The area of the capital has been reduced. Washington, D.C., no longer includes land in Virginia except for the land along the banks of the Potomac.
3. East bank
4. About one mile (1.6 kilometers)
5. L'Enfant may have wanted to make it easy for visitors to find the centers of government by providing them with numerous streets that would lead them there. He may also have wanted to emphasize the importance of the White House and the Capitol as the centers of the government by having so many roads lead to these buildings.

CHAPTER 13

Worksheet 25

1. Appalachian Mountains
2. Travelers faced the difficulty of crossing the Appalachian Mountains and the fear of Indian attack.
3. Mohawk River
4. Ohio River
5. Potomac River

6. The new frontier had its own traditions and attitudes. Settlers lived in crude cabins on small plots of land. That land usually belonged to Indians, so there was always the chance for Indian attack. Some settlers looking for adventure and independence moved on when others arrived. Other settlers formed small communities together.

7. Westerners claimed Britain was encouraging Indian resistance to frontier settlements. After the Battle of Tippecanoe, Britain became allies of the Indians, which further inflamed anti-British feelings in the West.

Worksheet 26

1. Before: from 30° to 47° North latitude, and 67° to 95° West longitude; after: from 30° to 47° North latitude, and 67° to 112° West longitude

2. About two times greater

3. New Orleans

4. From the Atlantic coast in the east to the Rocky Mountains in the west

5. The mouth of the Mississippi River

6. Spain

7. All of the major river systems between the Mississippi River and the Rocky Mountains

8. An area of such great size would offer natural resources, land for development and creation of states, and give the United States more control over the continent. Risks might include possible rebellion in new territories, and the burden of defending the new land.

CHAPTER 14

Worksheet 27

1. Toledo, Cincinnati

2. About 363 miles

3. Four

4. The Erie Canal and the Wabash and Erie Canal

5. The Illinois and Michigan Canal

6. The Wabash and Erie Canal

7. The Pennsylvania Canal and the Erie Canal

8. The Erie Canal

9. Ohio; the Ohio and Erie Canal, the Miami and Erie Canal, the Wabash and Erie Canal

10. The Ohio and Susquehanna rivers

11. He would send it north up the Mississippi River to the Ohio River. The crop would be shipped east along the Ohio River to Portsmouth. Then the crop would travel north on the Ohio and Erie Canal until it reached Cleveland.

Worksheet 28

1. The eastern region

2. Southeastern Virginia

3. Louisiana, Mississippi, Alabama, Georgia, South Carolina

4. Nebraska Territory

5. Slaves were involved in other parts of the Southern economy; slaves lived in areas where cotton was not a major crop or was not grown at all.

6. In areas of major cotton production, slaves often made up more than half of the population, since cotton production was extremely labor intensive. An exception was eastern Virginia where slaves made up more than half the population in 1860, although little cotton was grown there.

CHAPTER 15

Worksheet 29

1. At the parallel 36° 30', Missouri's southern border. The Compromise allowed Maine to be admitted as a free state and Missouri as a slave state to maintain the balance between free and slave states in Congress.

2. Missouri, Kentucky, Virginia, Maryland, Delaware

3. Unorganized Territory

4. Arkansas Territory and Florida Territory

5. The Seminole crossed the Gulf of Mexico to Louisiana. Then they headed north through Mississippi into Arkansas, and west across Arkansas to the Indian Territory.

6. About 750 miles (1207 kilometers)

7. From Georgia through Tennessee, Kentucky, Illinois, Missouri, and Arkansas

8. It did not put an end to sectionalism.

Worksheet 30

1. Maine, New York, Maryland

2. 139,222

3. 79

4. New York, Pennsylvania; the North

5. Adams's support was strongest in New England and the Middle Atlantic states, with the exception of Pennsylvania; Jackson's support was strongest in the South and the West.

6. The slave states had 114 electoral votes. In 1828, 131 electoral votes constituted a majority. Therefore, slave states did not have a majority of electoral votes.

7. As the population moved westward, the West's influence on national politics increased. As the population grew, the number of the western electoral votes increased.

CHAPTER 16

Worksheet 31

1. Minnesota, Wisconsin, and Illinois
2. Boston, New York, Brooklyn, Newark, Philadelphia, Baltimore, Cincinnati, Chicago, St. Louis, New Orleans
3. Connecticut, Kentucky, Louisiana, Texas
4. In the South
5. 0–1 percent; 2–4 percent
6. Many German immigrants settled in the countryside of the Midwest, while most Irish immigrants settled in the cities and outlying areas of the Northeast.
7. Many factors pushed people out of Europe in the mid–1800s, including overcrowding, poor harvests, famine, lack of work, and religious and ethnic persecution. Likewise, many factors pulled immigrants to America, including economic opportunity in the form of jobs and land, and freedom.

Worksheet 32

1. Canada
2. About 300 miles (483 kilometers)
3. They would take boats north across Lake Michigan and east across Lake Huron to Canada.
4. They could try to follow the sea route along the Atlantic coast to cities in the North.
5. Mexico, and through Florida to the Everglades and the Bahamas
6. The Cherokee in the Indian Territory supported slavery.
7. It would have been hardest to escape from states in the Deep South because slaves would have had a long way to travel.

CHAPTER 17

Worksheet 33

1. Oregon Trail: Fort Vancouver, Oregon; Santa Fe Trail: Santa Fe, New Mexico
2. Travelers might have come to the Mississippi River, then traveled by the Mississippi and Missouri rivers to Independence.
3. Mormon Trail; Nauvoo, Illinois
4. Oregon Trail; Platte River, Snake River, Columbia River
5. Santa Fe: end point for Santa Fe Trail, starting point for Old Spanish Trail
6. California Trail; it branched off the Oregon Trail before Ft. Hall.
7. Oregon Trail

8. A separate arm of the Santa Fe Trail branched off in order to pass through Bent's Fort.
9. The name probably dates back to the time when Mexico, a Spanish territory, controlled much of the American Southwest.

Worksheet 34

1. California, Nevada, and Utah
2. New Mexico
3. Arizona
4. Texas
5. 1876
6. Six
7. Statehood was a function of population. (Nevada, an exception, was brought into the Union during the Civil War.) Some of the states had resources that attracted large numbers of settlers, while others did not. The discovery of gold in California, for example, attracted many people to the area. States such as Arizona and New Mexico had few resources and large native populations which may have discouraged prospective settlers.

CHAPTER 18

Worksheet 35

1. Missouri
2. Twelve
3. At the latitude 36°30′N
4. California; slave state
5. The question of slavery would be decided by popular sovereignty.
6. Kentucky, Virginia, Tennessee
7. 17 states and part of New Jersey; no
8. South Carolina

Worksheet 36

1. Island
2. Charleston, Charleston Harbor
3. Ashley River, Cooper River
4. Two; Fort Moultrie, Fort Johnson
5. Gun batteries, areas of soldiers armed with heavy artillery
6. Confederate positions surrounding Fort Sumter could fire on it from all sides.
7. Main ship channel
8. The islands are honeycombed with marshes and inlets from the harbor. Union forces could probably not have set up an effective battle line in this terrain.
9. There is only one way to reach the fort, and the narrow channel is easy to defend. The Union ships were not warships but supply ships and would probably have been destroyed.

CHAPTER 19

Worksheet 37

1. Confederacy
2. Lee commanded the Confederate forces; Meade commanded the Union forces.
3. Texas
4. The areas around Jacksonville, St. Augustine, and Pensacola were under Union control.
5. About four months; about 350 miles (563 kilometers)
6. All Confederate ports on both the Gulf of Mexico and the Atlantic Ocean were blockaded.
7. Chattanooga
8. Lee traveled through Virginia, West Virginia, Maryland, and Pennsylvania.
9. Grant traveled through Georgia, South Carolina, and North Carolina.

Worksheet 38

1. The North
2. The supplies would head northeast and then north into Virginia to a railroad just south of Richmond. Then they would head southwest to Chattanooga and then northwest to Nashville.
3. About 800 miles (1287 kilometers); about 430 miles (692 kilometers)
4. The South lacked a good system of connections for its railroads. It also had few east–west routes. Without good connections, it would take longer for the South to move its men and supplies to the battle fronts. With few east–west routes, damage to any one of these routes would make it difficult to keep the soldiers supplied. The South's weak network of railroad would be responsible for the loss of battles and lives.

CHAPTER 20

Worksheet 39

1. 13
2. 17; 18
3. Tilden
4. South Carolina, Florida, Louisiana
5. Hayes
6. Tilden
7. Tilden originally had more undisputed electoral votes, and he might have been angered by the Compromise of 1877 in which Hayes was elected President in return for removing troops from the south.

Worksheet 40

1. The North
2. Texas, Louisiana, Mississippi, Georgia, South Carolina; cotton and the slavery system
3. All of them
4. Massachusetts, Connecticut, Rhode Island, New Jersey; these states occupied the same position after the war.
5. Kentucky
6. West Virginia, Nebraska, Kansas
7. The South
8. Most Confederate states moved from among the wealthiest before the war to among the least wealthy after the war.
9. The war was fought mostly on southern soil, so the South suffered far more devastation. The destruction of farmland ruined the South's agricultural economy. The North profited from the industries which sprang up to supply its army.

CHAPTER 21

Worksheet 41

1. New York Central, Pennsylvania
2. Central Pacific, Union Pacific
3. Chicago; San Francisco
4. Three
5. **a.** 2:00 P.M.   **b.** 1:00 P.M.   **c.** 3:00 P.M.
6. Chicago
7. About 450 miles (720 km)

Worksheet 42

1. About 1,250
2. 1890
3. About 300,000; about 400,000
4. 1894
5. **a.** Railroad Strike of 1877   **b.** Homestead Strike against the Carnegie Steel Company **c.** Pullman Strike against the Pullman Palace Car Company
6. It more than doubled from about 300,000 to about 700,000.
7. Students may suggest that railroad strikes would have crippled trade and transportation around the country, and caused prices on goods to rise. Students should note that the Railroad Strike of 1877 was ended by state and federal troops and the Pullman Strike of 1894 was ended by federal troops enforcing a court order to end the boycott.

CHAPTER 22

Worksheet 43

1. Chicago, Buffalo
2. Michigan, Wisconsin
3. Iron and steel
4. Mississippi River
5. Shipping on Lake Erie, railroad, road
6. By railroad or by road
7. They were shipping ports and they were linked by railroads or roads.
8. It has a Great Lakes port and a railroad center. It was linked to other cities by east-west routes as well as by north-south routes.

Worksheet 44

1. 33.6 million
2. Between 1891 and 1920
3. From northern, central, and western Europe
4. 8 percent, 63 percent
5. They are unshaded.
6. 81 percent, 25 percent
7. After 1890, most European immigrants came from southern and eastern Europe rather than from northern, central, and western Europe. Cities offered jobs in expanding industries. Cities contained ethnic neighborhoods where immigrants could receive assistance, speak their native language, and preserve their culture and traditions. Political machines in cities also helped immigrants.

CHAPTER 23

Worksheet 45

1. To drive cattle north from Texas to railroads from which they were shipped to eastern cities
2. San Antonio
3. Goodnight-Loving Trail
4. Dodge City, Ogallala
5. Goodnight-Loving and Western trails
6. Cheyenne, Ogallala
7. About 700 miles (1,120 km)

Worksheet 46

1. Mountains
2. Region 11: Mojave, Sonoran, and Chihuahuan deserts
3. Seven; western Great Plains, Rocky Mountains, Colorado Plateau, Basin and Mountain Range, Sierra Nevada, Central Valley, Pacific Coast
4. a. Rocky Mountains   b. Colorado Plateau   c. Basin and Mountain Range   d. Cascade Mountains

5. Black Hills
6. Approximately 100°W longitude
7. It was once ruled by Spain.
8. The Great Plains were full of buffalo. Gold and silver deposits lured many settlers to the Pacific Coast, Black Hills, Rocky Mountains, and Basin and Mountain Range regions. Minerals also attracted settlers to the Columbia Plateau and the Colorado Plateau regions. The Pacific Coast region had vast forests that sparked the lumbering industry. Railroads carried the great resources of the region to the east.

CHAPTER 24

Worksheet 47

1. Wyoming, 1869
2. The West
3. Pennsylvania, Maryland, West Virginia, Virginia, North Carolina, South Carolina, Georgia, Alabama
4. The Nineteenth Amendment
5. New York City
6. The West and the South
7. Wisconsin
8. Democratic Party, Woodrow Wilson; Progressive Party, Theodore Roosevelt; Republican Party, William Howard Taft
9. 8 electoral votes; two states

Worksheet 48

1. Northeast and Midwest
2. New York and Philadelphia
3. Seven
4. Seven
5. The South
6. Pittsburgh
7. Expansion of American industry, immigration, and settlement of the West caused the rapid growth of cities in the late 1800s. Immigrants and people from rural America moved to cities to work in expanding industries. Cities grew fastest in industrial regions where it was easy to bring together resources and labor.

CHAPTER 25

Worksheet 49

1. Mexico
2. The Bahamas
3. Haiti and Dominican Republic
4. Nicaragua
5. Cuba
6. Costa Rica
7. Venezuela

8. Guantanamo, on the island of Cuba

9. U.S. businesses found they could buy food and materials cheaply from Latin America, ship the goods to the U.S., and sell them for higher prices as American demand grew. They also bought large amounts of land in Latin America for farming and mining, using Latin Americans as a cheap source of labor.

Worksheet 50

1. About 50 miles (80 kilometers)
2. Six
3. Colón and Cristóbal; Panama City and Balboa
4. Southeast
5. 85 feet
6. Chagres River
7. Continental Divide
8. A hot, humid climate and disease-carrying mosquitoes hindered work on the canal. The canal could not be build at sea level, and the Continental Divide blocked construction. Workers first had to drain swamps to rid the area of mosquitoes and thus help control disease. Engineers built locks to raise and lower ships between different water levels. They dammed the Chagres River to control flooding. The Gaillard Cut opened a passageway through the Continental Divide.

CHAPTER 26

Worksheet 51

1. Boston
2. Midwest—Ohio
3. The Northeast—New England
4. Ohio Gang; they were people loyal to Harding from his years in Ohio politics.
5. Wyoming
6. New York; No one had ever flown nonstop across the Atlantic alone.
7. Detroit
8. New Orleans
9. Tennessee

Worksheet 52

1. Thick, solid black line
2. 1921; land east of Jordan River and Dead Sea became Transjordan, closed to Jewish settlement. 1923: land northeast of Sea of Galilee given to French Mandate for Syria.
3. About 260 miles (416 kilometers)
4. About 70 miles (112 kilometers)
5. Mediterranean Sea, Sea of Galilee, Jordan River, Dead Sea, Gulf of Aqaba
6. Transjordan

7. Mediterranean coast, access to Red Sea through Gulf of Aqaba
8. Palestine lay at the crossroads of routes such as the Suez Canal that connected the various parts of the British Empire. Control of Palestine helped Britain maintain control over those routes and its empire.

CHAPTER 27

Worksheet 53

1. Tennessee, Kentucky, Virginia, North Carolina, Georgia, Alabama, Mississippi
2. Tennessee; Alabama
3. Montana, North Dakota, South Dakota, Wyoming, Nebraska, Colorado, Kansas, Oklahoma, Texas, New Mexico, Iowa, Missouri
4. Kansas, Colorado, Oklahoma, Texas, New Mexico
5. California
6. Highway 66 and Highway 30
7. The Bonus Army was a protest group of WWI veterans that demanded early payment of their bonuses during the Depression. The veterans marched to Washington, D.C. in 1932 and set up camp there to pressure Congress.

Worksheet 54

1. South Carolina
2. The South; the South
3. New England
4. Farm tenancy remained roughly the same in Oregon, California, and Arizona, but increased in the rest of the West.
5. Declined; the maps show that the number of tenant farmers increased, indicating hard times for farmers. It is likely that many farmers gave up in the face of economic trouble.
6. A farm tenancy map for 1936 would probably show an increase in farm tenancy in the Great Plains states. Drought would have hurt farmers' incomes. Many of them would have been forced to turn their land over to banks and become tenant farmers.

CHAPTER 28

Worksheet 55

1. The growth in immigration that began in the late 1800s and the migration of large numbers of African Americans in the South to the North forced Americans to struggle with the identity of the nation.
2. Northern and western Europe

3. After 1860, immigrants from southern and eastern Europe and from Asia began arriving in the United States.

4. In cities along the East Coast, the Great Lakes, and the coast of California

5. New York City

6. Discrimination against Jews; Jews helped themselves by enrolling in night schools, public schools, colleges and universities. They became leaders in business, banking, the movie industry, and other professions.

7. While some European immigrants often faced discrimination because they were not Protestant, they assimilate and succeed because they were white. Because of their race, Asian immigrants could not do this.

Worksheet 56

1. About 685,000

2. About 160,000

3. The immigration laws reduced the number of immigrants from southern and eastern Europe. By the end of the 1920s, immigration from southern and eastern Europe was far less than it had been in 1914.

4. The number grew.

5. After the Act of 1924 went into effect

6. About 860,000

7. About 160,000

8. They greatly reduced total immigration.

9. During the 1920s many Americans opposed immigration, especially immigration from southern and eastern Europe. Racism, religious prejudice, fear of competition for jobs, and worries about immigrants' political views fed hostility towards foreigners. People often oppose immigration in times of political or economic uncertainty.

CHAPTER 29

Worksheet 57

1. Great Britain, Soviet Union

2. Sweden, Ireland, Switzerland, Spain, Portugal, Turkey

3. Axis forces occupied northern France; southern France was controlled by the Vichy French.

4. Germany, Italy

5. The Allies moved east from Normandy, France, through Axis-occupied territory; the Soviet Army moved west into Axis-occupied territory.

6. English Channel

7. The distance from the British coast to Calais is shorter than that between Britain and Normandy; Germany may have assumed a large assault would take the shortest crossing.

Worksheet 58

1. Libya, part of Tunisia, part of Egypt, France, Italy, Albania, Greece

2. Suez Canal

3. About 150 miles; El Alamein; October 23,1942

4. They landed on the western coast of North Africa and began moving east.

5. About seven months; in northern Tunisia; May 12, 1943

6. Italy and Sicily formed the "underbelly," the best access to the continent. Italy, an Axis nation, was accessible from Tunisia in North Africa. Two months after their victory in Tunisia, the Allies landed on Sicily. Two months later they were on the Italian mainland.

CHAPTER 30

Worksheet 59

1. Mekong River

2. Laos and Cambodia

3. South China Sea

4. Gulf of Tonkin

5. Hanoi, Haiphong

6. Saigon

7. About 60 miles

8. In and around Saigon, along the coast

9. Much of the interior part of the country

Worksheet 60

1. Three: Albania, Bulgaria, Yugoslavia

2. East Germany and China

3. Poland and East Germany were the most populous; Mongolia was the least populous.

4. The total population of Communist nations in Asia

5. Rumania, Hungary, Czechoslovakia, Poland

6. Communist governments were making gains in Eastern Europe and Asia. The number of people who lived in Communist states was increasing dramatically.

CHAPTER 31

Worksheet 61

1. Arizona, Florida, Nevada

2. New Hampshire, New Jersey, Michigan, Virginia

3. Connecticut, Delaware, Maryland

4. Massachusetts, New York, North Carolina, South Carolina, Georgia, Alabama, Mississippi, Rhode Island, Maine

5. 16–34 percent; Michigan and Pennsylvania; Michigan increased its population by 35–50 percent while Pennsylvania had a 0–15 percent gain.

6. Maine, Massachusetts, New York, Rhode Island, Vermont, Pennsylvania

Worksheet 62

1. 1790
2. Statement C is correct.
3. West Virginia
4. Washington, D.C.
5. Indiana
6. 1980
7. West and south
8. About 750 miles (1,200 kilometers)
9. (a) The discovery of gold drew thousands of people west, moving the population center west. **(b)** The completion of the transcontinental railroad made it easier for people to go west, hastening the shift westward. **(c)** The droughts discouraged people from moving west to farm, slowing the movement of the population center.

CHAPTER 32

Worksheet 63

1. Montgomery, Alabama
2. Topeka, Kansas; *Brown v. Board of Education*
3. Little Rock, Arkansas
4. Greensboro, North Carolina
5. Congress of Racial Equality (CORE)
6. It barred states from using different voting standards for blacks and whites, made discrimination in public places illegal, gave the federal government the power to integrate public schools and protect voting rights, and banned job discrimination based on race, sex, or religion.
7. He organized farm workers into a union, urged workers to strike when farm owners refused to deal with the union, and organized a consumer boycott of products harvested by non-union workers.

Worksheet 64

1. Delaware, 1953
2. Arkansas, Missouri, West Virginia, Texas: 1954; Florida, Virginia: 1959
3. Washington, D.C.

4. Louisiana, Mississippi, Alabama, Georgia, South Carolina
5. Oklahoma, Missouri, Kentucky, Delaware, Maryland
6. Over 50 percent
7. Louisiana, Mississippi, Alabama, Georgia, South Carolina; these states are located in the Deep South in the old "Cotton Kingdom," where there had been heavy concentrations of slaves before the Civil War. The legal separation of the races in this area had the weight of history behind it and made integration even more difficult.

CHAPTER 33

Worksheet 65

1. Lebanon; Syria and Jordan
2. Iran, Iraq, Kuwait, Saudi Arabia, Bahrain, Qatar, United Arab Emirates
3. Egypt; Mediterranean Sea and Red Sea
4. Iraq
5. The UN voted to use force to remove Iraqi troops. The United States and its allies began bombing Baghdad in January 1991. A month later they attacked Iraqi troops in Kuwait, freeing Kuwait in 100 hours.
6. Yugoslavia
7. Somalia
8. South Africa

Worksheet 66

1. Canada; Mexico
2. The North American Free Trade Agreement (NAFTA)
3. By creating the largest trading bloc in the world, NAFTA demonstrated how rising competition for markets and companies with jobs created the need for lower tariffs. Lower tariffs bring greater trade, as well as a greater risk that jobs will be lost to foreign competition.
4. The United States led the military effort, supplying most of the soldiers for the force.
5. Self-rule
6. The PLO slowly recognized Israel's right to exist. Israel agreed to talks on the occupied territories of the West Bank and Gaza. Israeli Prime Minister Rabin and PLO leader Arafat signed an agreement in 1993 calling for limited self-rule for part of the West Bank, as well as for Gaza.
7. Nelson Mandela and F. W. de Klerk were awarded the Nobel Peace Prize in 1993 for their work to bring democracy to South Africa.

8. The world faces the threat of global warming, an increase in the earth's temperature caused by the burning of fossil fuels. Some scientists believe global warming could wipe out species and flood lowlands. The world also faces the threat of deforestation, which destroys trees that clean the air and species that live in the rainforests. In 1990, the Clean Air Act was passed in the U.S. to reduce poisonous chemicals in the air. Also, an Earth Summit was held in Brazil in 1992 to discuss environmental challenges.